AI and Genealogy: A Practical Guide to Summarizing, Transcribing, and Translating Historical Documents

by Thomas MacEntee

Table of Contents

AI and Genealogy A Practical Guide to Summarizing, Transcribing, and Translating Historical Records

Preface

Genealogical research has always called for a deep dive into a wide array of historical resources—everything from centuries-old marriage registers and immigration documents to handwritten diaries and newspaper clippings that capture the rhythm of our ancestors' daily lives. And let's be honest: it wasn't that long ago that we, as researchers, had to wade through every line ourselves, painstakingly summarizing, transcribing, and, in some cases, translating these materials with nothing but our own eyes, our own expertise, and a whole lot of patience.

But things have changed—and in a big way. Thanks to cutting-edge Artificial Intelligence (AI), genealogists now have powerful new tools at their fingertips. These advanced language models can take your family documents—no matter how large, how old, or how challenging to read—and deliver concise summaries, transcriptions, and translations with impressive accuracy. From hobbyist family historians to seasoned professionals, this technology can truly turbocharge your workflow and open up new research frontiers.

This book is here to help you cut through the hype and get right to the heart of what AI can do for your genealogy projects. We'll explore how these new tools work, walk you through today's best AI platforms, and lay out clear, practical strategies so you can quickly start applying them to your own research. Bottom line? If you use AI intelligently and ethically, you'll unlock new possibilities in your genealogy work that you might never have dreamed possible.

AI and Genealogy A Practical Guide to Summarizing, Transcribing, and Translating Historical Records

Chapter 1: Understanding the Core Concepts of AI for Genealogy

When it comes to modern genealogy, we're often juggling a variety of historical documents—census returns, parish registers, diaries, immigration forms, legal papers, and more. Each record type has its own quirks and challenges: unusual terms that have fallen out of use, handwriting that's tough to decipher, and documents that may have seen better days. With artificial intelligence (AI) now at our fingertips, we have a new set of tools to help us work through these complexities, letting us pull information more quickly, interpret data more accurately, and even translate foreign-language materials with greater ease. But to make the most of these advancements, it's important to get a good handle on the core AI concepts—how they work, what they can do, and how to apply them to your own genealogy research.

This chapter takes you on a guided tour of the foundational AI tools and concepts you'll likely encounter: natural language processing (NLP), optical character recognition (OCR), machine translation (MT), and large language models (LLMs). We'll also talk about how important it is to keep historical and cultural context in mind when using these technologies. Armed with this knowledge, you'll be able to spot the right tools for your project, ask better questions that yield richer results, and seamlessly integrate AI into a solid, time-tested research strategy.

Defining Artificial Intelligence and Its Relevance to Genealogy

When most of us think about technology and genealogy, we usually picture online databases, digitized records, and DNA tests. But there's a new player in town that's been making waves well beyond the genealogy sphere: Artificial Intelligence, or AI. At its core, AI involves getting computers to "think" like humans—to learn, reason, and make decisions. While AI can appear in many forms like robots or image recognition tools, this book focuses on those AI technologies that help us understand and work with text. That's right—these are the tools that can summarize, transcribe, and translate the very documents that genealogists often find so challenging.

If you've spent any time researching, you know that family history documents can be as diverse as the ancestors we're researching. One day you're deciphering a handwritten parish register from 18th-century Bavaria; the next, you're puzzling over an early 1900s immigrant's letter written in old-fashioned Italian. Sorting through all that text takes time, patience, and specialized skills. This is where AI comes into play. By harnessing cutting-edge language technologies, genealogists can:

- **Process Massive Amounts of Data:** AI can "read" through long, detailed records—documents you'd spend hours or even days analyzing—and present the highlights in minutes.

- **Make Records More Accessible:** Struggling with faded handwriting or foreign-language records? AI can help convert scribbles into searchable text and seamlessly translate words that once stopped you cold.

- **Reduce Research Time:** Instead of sifting through every page, genealogists can let AI handle the heavy lifting. You can then spend more time putting those puzzle pieces together into a meaningful family story.

Natural Language Processing and Language Models

The branch of AI that helps machines understand and generate human language is called Natural Language Processing (NLP). Think of NLP as the interpreter that helps your computer "read" text-based content. Whether it's tagging parts of speech, summarizing a long will, extracting a birth date from a church register, or translating a German newspaper announcement, NLP makes it possible.

In recent years, NLP has grown by leaps and bounds thanks to Large Language Models (LLMs). These powerful systems have been trained on vast amounts of text—everything from classic literature to obscure legal documents. They excel at spotting patterns and relationships between words, which means they can produce human-like summaries, handle tricky translations, and adapt to historical documents. For genealogists, that's huge. LLMs can:

- **Identify Key Details:** Quickly pinpoint names, places, dates, and other essentials that matter in family history.

- **Summarize Complex Text:** Tackle entire books of local history or property records and give you a clear "CliffsNotes" version.

- **Interpret Old or Unusual Language:** While not perfect, today's models are much better at dealing with archaic terms and spelling quirks, especially if you give them some context.

Summarization: Getting Right to the Good Stuff

Ever spent hours combing through a lengthy document, just to find one small but critical detail? Summarization tools can save you that headache. They distill lengthy text into its core points, making it easier to identify what's worth exploring further. With AI doing the grunt work, you can:

- **Condense Huge Texts:** Turn a 100-page county history into a few paragraphs to see if it's worth reading in full.

- **Highlight Important Events:** Pinpoint births, marriages, migrations, and other life events in a long family biography.

- **Streamline Your Workflow:** Use AI's quick summaries to figure out which documents deserve a deeper look.

Transcription: From Handwritten Scrawl to Searchable Text

For many genealogists, transcription has been a lifelong nemesis. Old handwritten documents, faded ink, and long-forgotten abbreviations can slow you down. Enter AI-powered transcription. This goes beyond old-school OCR technology, which mainly worked with printed text. Today's AI can tackle handwriting—sometimes even the trickiest "chicken scratch." When you adopt these tools, you'll:

- **Search Content Instantly:** Once transcribed, documents become keyword searchable. No more squinting at tiny script!

- **Improve Accuracy Over Time:** Many transcription tools learn from corrections, so they get better the more you use them.

- **Protect and Share:** Transcribing ancient documents turns fragile originals into digital, shareable text for others to enjoy.

Translation: Overcoming Language Barriers

If your ancestors traveled the globe, you know language can be a huge hurdle. AI-driven translation tools are more accurate and context-aware than older, clunky systems. They can handle old-fashioned terms and place names—especially if you give them some background. This opens a world of opportunity:

- **Access More Records:** Don't let language limit your research. Now you can use sources from other countries and cultures.

- **Understand Cultural Nuances:** Good translations go beyond word-for-word rendering. They help you catch the social, cultural, or historical significance behind those words.

- **Connect with Researchers Worldwide:** Share your findings with cousins and collaborators who speak different languages.

Context and Prompting: The Key to Better Results

AI can't read your mind—it relies on what you tell it. The prompts and context you provide can make all the difference. Is this an 1820s Norwegian church record? A WWII-era postcard from a French soldier? The more detail you supply, the better the AI's results.

- **Give Time Frames and Locations:** Setting the stage helps the AI guess meanings of archaic words or old-fashioned names.

- **State Your Goals:** Are you looking for births and marriages, or property holdings? Be clear about what you need.

Know the Limits and Keep it Ethical

While AI is a game-changer, it's not foolproof. Sometimes it "hallucinates" facts that aren't there. Poor image quality, very old scripts, and certain languages can still stump it. And remember, historical documents can contain sensitive content. AI might inadvertently reflect biases or misunderstand them. Always:

- **Cross-Check Results:** AI is a helper, not a replacement for your own good judgment.

- **Be Mindful of Sensitive Topics:** Handle potentially delicate information with care.

Setting Yourself Up for AI-Enhanced Success

Before diving in, take some time to understand how AI works and think about what you want to accomplish. You'll still rely on your own genealogical expertise—AI just speeds up the grunt work. By using AI wisely and ethically, you can uncover your family's story faster and with more confidence than ever.

With the groundwork laid, you're ready to explore the tools and techniques that will transform your research process. Get comfortable with these concepts now, and you'll soon wonder how you ever did genealogy without a little help from AI.

* * *

In the coming chapters, we'll take the next steps together, building on these basics and applying them to your own genealogy projects. We'll walk through some of today's top AI platforms, discover how to efficiently summarize large text collections, tackle difficult handwriting and faded documents, and even translate sources from languages that might otherwise feel like roadblocks. As you blend solid research principles with these emerging technologies, you'll gain the skills needed to uncover and safeguard your family's most meaningful stories, ensuring they stand the test of time.

Chapter 2: Surveying the Leading AI Platforms for Genealogical Research

As more and more genealogists tap into the power of artificial intelligence (AI) to supercharge their family history work, we're seeing a flood of new tools hit the market. Each one has its own strengths, quirks, and pricing options. Some tools shine at boiling down long documents into manageable highlights, while others tackle tough tasks like deciphering handwriting from centuries past or bridging language gaps by translating old records. The trick is figuring out which tool best fits both the type of document you're digging into and the type of help you need.

In this chapter, we'll explore some of today's leading AI-powered platforms designed to help you summarize, transcribe, and translate historical materials. We'll get into the nitty-gritty of popular language models, check out which transcription services do the best job of turning scribbled scrawl into readable text, and see how integrated research assistants can streamline your overall process. We'll also talk costs and which situations call for which solutions. By getting a handle on how these tools stack up, you can put together a toolkit perfectly matched to your genealogical research needs.

ChatGPT (OpenAI)

Overview:

Developed by OpenAI, **ChatGPT** is one of the most well-known and widely used large language models. Renowned for its generative abilities, it can handle a broad range of tasks, including summarizing large documents, extracting key details from complex texts, generating translations, and providing contextual explanations. Its conversational interface makes it accessible to beginners and experts alike. While initially famous for free public access, ChatGPT now offer paid plans (ChatGPT Plus and Enterprise) that provides enhanced features such as higher-quality responses, faster response times, and the ability to handle larger context windows.

Key Features:

- **Versatile Prompting:** ChatGPT, developed by OpenAI, responds to user prompts by generating text based on patterns it has learned from extensive training data.

- **Summarization and Translation:** It excels at summarizing long documents—books, articles, genealogical guides—and can provide serviceable translations for many modern languages.

- **Context-Aware Assistance:** Through iterative prompting, you can guide the model to improve the accuracy of its output. If the initial translation or summary is unclear, providing more context and constraints helps refine the results.

Strengths for Genealogists:

- **User-Friendly Interface:** ChatGPT's chat-based format makes it easy for newcomers to AI to interact naturally.

- **Rapid Summaries:** Extracting key points from large PDF documents or web-based texts is straightforward.

- **Initial Translation Attempts:** While not specialized in historical texts, ChatGPT can offer a first-pass translation that you can refine.

Limitations:

- **Context Dependency:** Performance improves significantly with detailed context. Without historical or cultural cues, the model may misinterpret archaic terms.

- **Occasional Hallucinations:** ChatGPT can sometimes produce inaccurate or overly confident statements, requiring human review.

Pricing:

- **Free Tier:** A basic version is available at no cost but may have limited capabilities or slower response times.

- **Paid Plans (ChatGPT Plus and Enterprise):** Offer faster responses, priority access during peak times, and more advanced models (like GPT-4), increasing accuracy and reasoning.

Claude (Anthropic)

Overview:

Claude, developed by Anthropic, is another advanced language model with a strong emphasis on user safety, honesty, and helpfulness. Its architecture and training regimen were designed to reduce harmful outputs and encourage more reliable assistance. Claude is often praised for its ability to handle complex instructions and produce organized, coherent results. This makes it an attractive option for genealogists dealing with intricate archival materials.

Key Features:

- **Long-Context Handling:** Claude is known for handling longer input contexts than many of its competitors, making it valuable for very long genealogical texts such as full-length books or multi-volume records.

- **Dialogue-Based Summarization:** Similar to ChatGPT, Claude uses a conversational interface, but its training emphasizes producing less biased and more "safe" outputs.

Strengths for Genealogists:

- **Complex Document Summaries:** Ideal when you need to distill extensive genealogical publications into bite-sized overviews.

- **Reduced Toxicity and Bias:** Claude's training focuses on producing more balanced and appropriate responses, which may be beneficial when interpreting sensitive historical documents that touch on cultural or religious subjects.

Limitations:

- **Less Widely Integrated:** Claude might be less commonly integrated into genealogy software ecosystems, requiring more manual workflows.

- **Still Developing Historical Specializations:** While strong at summarization, specialized historical or linguistic models for Claude are still emerging.

Pricing:

- **API and Third-Party Tools:** Claude's cost varies depending on platform integration and usage through partners. Some services may offer limited free trials or credits, while others require a paid subscription or pay-as-you-go model.

Copilot (Microsoft web version)

Overview:

Microsoft Copilot, as deployed in web-based environments, represents Microsoft's effort to bring the power of large language models and AI-driven assistance directly into familiar, browser-accessible tools. Although implementations vary depending on the product ecosystem—such as Microsoft 365 web apps, Bing, and Edge—the overarching goal is to streamline work, improve productivity, and elevate user experiences through AI-

AI and Genealogy A Practical Guide to Summarizing, Transcribing, and Translating Historical Records

generated insights, drafting assistance, and data analysis within a web interface.

Key Features:

- **Seamless Integration into Microsoft 365 Web Apps:** Microsoft 365 Copilot is designed to work directly within the web-based versions of Microsoft's productivity tools—Word Online, Excel Online, PowerPoint Online, and Outlook on the web—without requiring desktop installations. This means genealogists can access AI-driven assistance from virtually anywhere, using only a web browser and their Microsoft 365 account.

- **Intelligent Document Summarization:** When working with large genealogical documents stored in OneDrive or SharePoint, Copilot can create concise summaries that highlight key information, such as family names, ancestral locations, or pertinent dates, all within the web-based interface of Word.

- **Context-Aware Support Across Your Workspace:** Copilot uses data from the Microsoft Graph, including documents, emails, and chat conversations associated with your Microsoft 365 account, to provide relevant suggestions. For example, if you have genealogical notes or research logs stored as Word files or Excel spreadsheets online, Copilot can incorporate these references to deliver more informed guidance.

Strengths for Genealogists:

- **No Installation Required:** Access Copilot's capabilities through a web browser on any device, perfect for traveling genealogists or those working from libraries and archives.

- **Efficient Research Workflow:** Summarize newly uploaded genealogy-related PDFs, quickly identify mentions of particular surnames or ancestral villages, or refine and reorganize data in Excel spreadsheets—all without leaving the web-based environment.

- **Collaboration Made Easy:** For research teams scattered across different locations, Copilot's integration into SharePoint and OneDrive ensures everyone can view, edit, and summarize documents in real-time, enhancing group projects and family history collaborations.

Limitations:

- **Requires Microsoft 365 Web Access:** Copilot's web-based version relies on Microsoft 365 subscriptions and online document storage. If your genealogical materials aren't in the Microsoft cloud ecosystem, you may need to migrate them for best results.

- **Not Specialized in Handwritten Document OCR:** While Copilot excels at summarizing and refining text content online, it cannot directly transcribe handwritten records. You must first use specialized OCR or transcription tools to generate searchable text for Copilot to interpret.

- **Accuracy Tied to Input Quality:** As with any AI tool, the more context you provide—such as historical background, document type, or known family details—the more useful and accurate Copilot's suggestions and summaries will be.

Pricing:

- **Available with Eligible Microsoft 365 Plans:** Copilot's web-based functionality is expected to be rolled out as a premium add-on to existing Microsoft 365 subscriptions. Pricing will vary depending on your plan and the level of features enabled, so

AI and Genealogy A Practical Guide to Summarizing, Transcribing, and Translating Historical Records

genealogists should check Microsoft's official pricing and feature announcements for the latest details.

Genesis (Google)

Overview:

Google's foray into AI-driven text understanding and generation—encompassed by tools like **Genesis** and upcoming large language models—builds upon the company's extensive expertise in search, indexing, translation, and OCR technology. While some aspects of Google's advanced AI tools remain in development or in limited release, their potential for genealogical research is substantial.

Key Features:

- **Google's Generative AI Efforts:** "Genesis" is part of Google's move into generative AI, potentially integrating advanced language models into its suite of services—Google Workspace, Google Cloud, and beyond.

- **Search Integration:** Future integrations with Google's search and cloud ecosystem could allow genealogists to leverage Google's OCR (via Google Drive), translation (Google Translate), and summarization tools seamlessly.

Strengths for Genealogists:

- **Seamless Ecosystem:** If integrated into Google services, it may allow you to upload documents to Google Drive, run OCR with Google Vision, summarize with Genesis, and then translate with Google Translate—all within one familiar platform.

- **Constant Updates and Research:** Google's heavy investment in AI research may lead to rapid improvements in accuracy, language support, and historical document handling.

Limitations:

- **Early Stage:** At the time of writing, Genesis is still emerging. Its capabilities, availability, and terms of use may change rapidly.

- **Specialization Uncertain:** It's unclear whether Genesis or related Google tools will specialize in historical handwriting or archaic languages any time soon.

Pricing:

- **Potentially Freemium:** Google may offer basic features for free (similar to Google Translate) with premium tiers or enterprise-level integrations for advanced functionality.

Perplexity

Overview:

- **Perplexity** is an AI-powered research assistant designed to answer queries, summarize documents, and provide sources. While it may not be as widely known as ChatGPT, Claude, or Google's offerings, Perplexity's strength lies in its ability to give well-sourced answers and encourage deeper exploration of topics, making it well-suited for genealogists who value traceability and source references.

Key Features:

- **Research Assistant:** Perplexity AI is designed as a research-oriented assistant that provides answers backed by citations. It excels at sourcing information from the web and summarizing it, making it useful for contextualizing historical data and verifying genealogical facts.

- **Concise Answers with References:** When you ask Perplexity a question about a place, historical event, or genealogical detail, it aims to provide concise answers with linked references.

Strengths for Genealogists:

- **Fact-Checking and Verification:** While Perplexity may not transcribe a handwritten ledger directly, it can help you understand historical context by quickly referencing multiple sources. For example, if you are unsure about the meaning of an occupation listed in a 19th-century census, Perplexity can help confirm details from external websites.

- **Supplementary Research Tool:** Use it in tandem with OCR and translation tools to verify and expand upon information found in documents.

Limitations:

- **Limited Document Handling:** Perplexity AI is less about direct transcription or translation and more about locating and summarizing web-accessible information. You must bring your own digitized texts.

- **Reliance on External Sources:** It depends on publicly accessible data; if historical documents aren't online or well-documented, Perplexity's answers may be limited.

Pricing:

- **Free to Use:** Perplexity currently offers a free interface, with potential future premium tiers for advanced features or integrations.

Transkribus

Overview

Transkribus is a comprehensive platform designed to facilitate the transcription, recognition, and analysis of written documents, particularly those that are historical, handwritten, or otherwise difficult to process using conventional text-recognition tools. It combines state-of-the-art **handwriting recognition** (HWR) technology, layout analysis, and machine learning techniques to help individuals, archives, libraries, and research institutions streamline their work with textual sources.

Key Features:

- **Handwritten Text Recognition (HTR) Specialization:** Transkribus is built specifically to handle historical handwriting. It uses AI models trained on thousands of archival documents, enabling more accurate transcription of cursive or mixed-type documents that often stymie standard OCR tools.

- **Model Training:** You can train custom models on your own corpus of documents. If your ancestors used a particular script style or your collection features consistent handwriting, custom training can dramatically improve accuracy over time.

- **Layout and Structure Recognition:** It can handle complex page layouts, margin notes, and annotations often present in genealogical records.

Strengths for Genealogists:

- **Historical Document Focus:** Perfect for extracting text from parish registers, diaries, old letters, and census sheets—types of documents at the heart of genealogical work.

- **Integration with Archives:** Many European archives and libraries recommend or integrate with Transkribus, making it easier to work directly with historical collections.

Limitations:

- **Limited Summarization and Translation:** Transkribus excels in transcription but is not designed for large-scale summarization or machine translation. You'll likely need to export its transcripts to other AI platforms for subsequent steps.

- **Learning Curve:** Understanding how to train and fine-tune models can be time-consuming for beginners.

Pricing:

- **Freemium Model:** A free tier is available for a limited number of pages. Additional credits or subscriptions are required for larger transcription projects or advanced features like model training and enhanced processing capabilities.

Selecting the Right Tool for the Task

Purpose of Your Task

- **For Summarization of Large Historical Texts:** ChatGPT and Claude shine due to their robust summarization capabilities and flexibility with prompts.

- **For Transcription Assistance (OCR/HTR Integration):** While none of these platforms provide OCR by themselves, you can use Google's **Vision AI** (not detailed above) or Adobe's OCR tools, then run the transcribed text through ChatGPT or Claude for cleanup. Genesis, when more fully integrated, may streamline the entire process if integrated with Google's document suite.

- **For Translation:** Google's ecosystem, powered by Google Translate and potentially integrated with Genesis, can provide top-tier translations. ChatGPT and Claude also offer nuanced translations if given proper historical and cultural context.

- **For Source-Backed Information and Exploration:** Perplexity provides references, helping you verify claims and discover additional resources. This is especially useful if you need leads on where to find original documents or secondary analyses.

- **For Structuring and Formatting Data:** Copilot can help format and prepare large bodies of text for databases, spreadsheets, or genealogical software.

Budget and Frequency of Use

- **Occasional Researcher:** A free or low-cost tool, like the free version of ChatGPT or Perplexity, may suffice.

- **Frequent or Professional Researcher:** Consider premium subscriptions or API integrations from ChatGPT Plus, Claude's advanced models, or Transkribus credits to handle larger volumes efficiently.

Technical Skills and Workflows

- **Non-Technical Users:** opts for user-friendly interfaces like ChatGPT or Transkribus' graphical interface.

- **Technical Users:** Integration with GitHub Copilot and APIs allows for custom pipelines that can automate repetitive tasks.

AI and Genealogy A Practical Guide to Summarizing, Transcribing, and Translating Historical Records

Integrating Multiple Platforms Into Your Workflow

Many genealogists find that using multiple platforms in tandem yields the best results. For instance, you might:

- **Begin with OCR:** Use Google Vision AI or a similar OCR tool to convert scanned documents into text.

- **Summarize the Text:** Feed the extracted text into ChatGPT or Claude for a concise summary highlighting genealogical details.

- **Verify Information and Find Sources:** Turn to Perplexity to discover additional documents, references, or related historical context.

- **Translate Key Passages:** Use Google Translate or ChatGPT's translation capabilities to understand texts written in foreign languages.

- **Format and Organize Data:** Employ Copilot to structure the transcribed and translated results into a well-organized dataset suitable for your genealogical software.

By leveraging the strengths of each platform, you can create a flexible, scalable, and accurate research pipeline that adapts to the varied challenges of genealogical research.

Cost Considerations and Resource Management

While some platforms offer generous free tiers, others require paid subscriptions or credits for extensive use. Consider the scope of your project, your budget, and the frequency of AI use:

- **Free Tiers:** Tools like ChatGPT, Claude, and Perplexity typically have free tiers that allow users to experiment with basic features. For smaller projects or occasional lookups, these may suffice.

- **Paid Subscriptions**: For more intensive research—such as summarizing entire books, frequently translating long documents, or performing multiple queries per day—investing in a paid subscription can provide more reliable access, faster response times, and enhanced capabilities.

- **Pay-Per-Use Models**: Some services charge based on the volume of data processed or the number of queries made. Such models can be economical if your usage is sporadic or seasonal.

As you continue to explore these platforms, keep track of your usage habits and their costs. By doing so, you can allocate your resources efficiently, ensuring that you receive the highest value for your investment.

Staying Current with Evolving Tools

The world of AI is evolving at a rapid pace. New models emerge frequently, existing platforms gain new features, and integrations with genealogical websites or archives may appear. To stay ahead of the curve:

- **Regularly Check Platform Updates**: Visit the official websites and documentation pages of these AI tools to stay informed about improvements, new features, and changes in pricing.

- **Join Genealogical Forums and Communities**: Online genealogical groups, forums, and social media communities often discuss new AI tools, offer tips for effective usage, and provide reviews of their experiences.

AI and Genealogy A Practical Guide to Summarizing, Transcribing, and Translating Historical Records

- **Experiment with Multiple Platforms:** Periodically test new platforms or updated versions of existing ones. This hands-on experimentation can reveal unexpected advantages or more seamless workflows.

* * *

Think of today's genealogical research landscape as a buffet of cutting-edge technologies—each one offering a different flavor to enhance your family history projects. With a plethora of AI tools now at our fingertips, the challenge isn't finding something that works, but choosing the right platform for the right task. ChatGPT and Claude can help distill a dense family narrative into concise summaries and translate foreign-language documents into something readable. Perplexity AI is all about speed and confirmation, quickly providing facts and citations to bolster your research. For those tough-to-read handwritten records, Transkribus turns scribbles into searchable text. And if you're ready to dive deeper into automation and coding, GitHub Copilot guides you through technical projects that once seemed out of reach. The real trick is understanding each tool's strengths, constraints, and pricing so you can assemble a tailored toolkit that takes your genealogy work to new heights.

As we move forward in this book, we won't just be talking theory—we'll roll up our sleeves and put these tools to the test in everyday research scenarios. We'll look at transcribing fragile parish registers, summarizing entire family histories into easy-to-reference nuggets of information, and even translating that elusive immigration record to shatter your research brick walls. Together, we'll discover how applying these cutting-edge resources can revolutionize the way you uncover, document, and share your ancestral story.

Chapter 3: Summarizing Large Documents

Ever find yourself staring down a massive text—maybe a thick local history volume, an old genealogy journal, a lengthy family narrative, or even a centuries-old account of your ancestors' homeland—wondering how you'll uncover the key details hidden inside? Let's face it: reading through hundreds of pages can drain your time and energy. This is where artificial intelligence steps in with a game-changing advantage. AI-powered summarization tools can quickly zero in on the names, themes, and must-have tidbits, letting you skip straight to the parts that matter most to your research.

In this chapter, we'll roll up our sleeves and dive deep into how you can harness AI to summarize large genealogical documents. We'll explore the nuts and bolts of different summarization methods, walk through prepping your materials for top-notch results, discuss how to give the AI the right guidance using context and prompts, and show you ways to confirm the accuracy of the summaries you get. By the end, you'll have a solid roadmap for turning those intimidating tomes into streamlined sources of genealogical gold.

Understanding Summarization Methods

- **Abstractive Summarization:** Abstractive summarization involves the AI producing a condensed version of the text using its own words. Rather than extracting exact sentences from the original document, the model synthesizes the core meaning. This approach can be more human-like and flexible, often capturing the essence of complex passages in a concise manner. However, it may introduce subtle inaccuracies or omit certain names if not guided properly.

- **Extractive Summarization:** Extractive summarization selects key sentences or phrases directly from the text. While this method ensures factual consistency with the original wording, the resulting summary may feel disjointed and less coherent. For genealogists, an extractive summary can still be valuable for identifying which pages or sections contain references to a specific ancestor, place, or event.

- **Hybrid Approaches:** Some AI tools combine both approaches—first identifying the most important segments and then generating a more coherent, human-readable abstract from them. This hybrid method can yield high-quality, contextually rich summaries that are both accurate and concise.

Preparing Documents for Summarization

Digitizing the Source

If the document you want to summarize is only available as a scanned image, start by converting it into machine-readable text using OCR tools (e.g., Transkribus for handwriting or Adobe Acrobat for printed text). High-quality input text improves summarization accuracy. Also consider using the OCR software included with the scanner.

For books and articles in PDF, also consider sources such as Google Books, Hathi Trust, and Internet Archive.

Cleaning and Formatting

Before feeding text into an AI summarizer, try to remove extraneous elements like page numbers, headers, footers, and repeated titles. Ensuring that the text is well-structured helps the AI identify coherent sections and understand context. In some cases, breaking very large documents into chapters or sections can yield better, more targeted summaries.

AI and Genealogy A Practical Guide to Summarizing, Transcribing, and Translating Historical Records

Providing Contextual Prompts

AI models perform better when given context. Before requesting a summary, explain the nature of the document, its time period, and why it matters. For example:

> *"This is a local history book about rural New York in the late 19th century.*
> *I am looking for information related to the Crawford family, their property holdings, and any mention of their participation in the community church."*

Techniques for Summarizing Large Documents

Chunking the Document

For lengthy files (hundreds of pages), break the text into manageable chunks—perhaps one chapter or 20-page segment at a time. Summarize each section separately, then ask the AI to create a high-level summary from these section-level summaries. This step-by-step approach can reduce information overload and maintain accuracy.

Layered Summaries:

You can create a hierarchy of summaries:

- **High-Level Summary:** Identifies main themes, time periods, and major family names.

- **Section Summaries:** Delve deeper into each chapter or subsection, highlighting more specific events, names, and date ranges.

- **Detail Extraction:** Once you identify the relevant sections, ask the AI to extract specific facts: birth dates, land records, marriage references, or immigration details.

By layering your approach, you can start broad and then focus more narrowly as you identify the sections of greatest interest.

Iterative Refinement

If the initial summary feels too vague or misses key details, refine your request. Add instructions like:

> *"Please revise the summary to highlight any mention of the Crawford family. Focus on names, dates, and property transactions between 1850 and 1900."*

This iterative process helps guide the AI toward more relevant and accurate outputs.

Choosing the Right Tool for Summarization

Different AI platforms have varying strengths. Consider the following:

- **ChatGPT or Claude:** Excellent general-purpose summarizers with strong language capabilities. They're well suited for producing readable, well-structured summaries.

- **Genesis (Google):** As Google's tools evolve, they may integrate smoothly with your Google Drive documents, simplifying the workflow.

- **Perplexity AI:** While primarily a research assistant, it can still provide concise overviews or guide you to key sections of text.

- **Microsoft 365 Copilot:** If you store documents in OneDrive or SharePoint, Copilot can produce summaries directly within Word Online, streamlining your research within a familiar environment.

Remember to test several tools to find which one best matches your documents and research style. You may find that ChatGPT excels at capturing narrative histories, while Claude might better handle dense academic texts.

Providing Contextual and Historical Details

For genealogical documents, historical context is crucial. AI tools trained primarily on modern text might struggle with archaic terms, outdated place names, or old-fashioned occupations. Add context to your prompt, such as:

- The time period covered by the document (e.g., "This text covers events in the late 18th century in rural Bavaria.")

- The type of document (e.g., "This is a local church history that lists parishioners and their community roles.")

- The desired focus (e.g., "Focus on mentions of the Müller family, their children's birth records, and any notes on their migration patterns.")

By doing so, you help the AI model zero in on relevant details and interpret historical nuances more accurately.

Verifying the Results

- **Cross-Referencing with the Original Text**: After receiving a summary, skim through the original document to confirm key facts. Did the AI correctly identify names, dates, and places? Are there inconsistencies or obvious errors? AI is a starting point, not a final authority.

- **Consulting External Databases and References**: If the summary mentions a location or historical event, verify it against known historical timelines, genealogical indexes, or reputable archives. Cross-referencing helps confirm that the summarized information is aligned with established historical facts.

- **Refine and Re-Request**: If you spot errors, correct them and run another query. For instance, if the AI misidentified a surname, explain that the name is spelled differently and ask it to re-check the text. This iterative correction loop can improve the accuracy of the final summary.

Practical Examples

Example 1: Summarizing a 57-Page Genealogy Book dated 1916 in PDF

- Break the book's text into sections of 20–30 pages.

- Ask ChatGPT to summarize each section, focusing on names, notable events, and locations mentioned.

- Compile all section summaries, then instruct the AI to create a top-level summary highlighting patterns—like the migration trends of a particular family line.

- If certain family names appear, request a separate summary detailing the frequency, context, and relevant events linked to them.

Extensive notes and test results can be found in **Appendix 3 – Summarizing Practical Example 1 – *The Genealogy of David Putman and His Descendants***.

Beyond Summarization: Next Steps

Once you have a summary highlighting key facts and figures, you can use it as a springboard for further research:

- **Targeted Translation:** If the document is in another language, you now know which sections are worth translating in detail.

- **Deeper Analysis:** Summaries can point you towards patterns—such as recurring locations or occupations—that warrant deeper investigation.

- **Integration with Family Tree Software:** Relevant data extracted from summaries (names, birth dates, migration events) can be added to your genealogical database or family tree software for future reference.

* * *

Think about it: using AI to summarize those massive genealogical documents you've been dreading can be a real game-changer. With the right prep work and the right tools, you can quickly size up a source and decide if it's worth a deeper dive. The trick? Give the AI some historical context to work with and keep fine-tuning your prompts until you get the best possible output. Over time, as you sharpen your skills at guiding the process and verifying the results, you'll discover that even the most complicated old records can yield meaningful insights—without all the usual hassle.

Chapter 4: Transcribing Historical Documents

Transcription is one of those essential skills that can make a world of difference in your genealogy research. It turns those tough-to-read documents—faded newspaper clippings, typed census sheets, scribbled diary pages, and old family letters—into text you can actually work with. Each record type has its own quirks: early newspapers might have ink that's barely there and columns that twist and turn, vital records sometimes mix tidy printed text with scrawled annotations, and those personal letters you inherited often feature challenging handwriting and outdated language that'll send you flipping through old dictionaries.

Thanks to recent advances in artificial intelligence, we're now seeing tools that can handle a lot of that tricky transcription work for us. Instead of squinting at spidery handwriting and guessing at every other word, you can rely on AI-driven OCR (optical character recognition) and handwriting recognition to do much of the heavy lifting. These cutting-edge models are trained on massive sets of historical texts and fonts, which means less time straining your eyes and more time putting that data to use in your family history projects.

In this chapter, we'll break down the core ideas behind AI-based transcription. I'll take you through the typical workflow, show you how to squeeze the best possible accuracy out of these tools, and then share some tips on weaving those freshly transcribed documents right back into your overall genealogy research plan. It's all about working smarter, not harder, to uncover the stories that connect you to your ancestors.

Understanding the Core Technologies Behind Transcription

Optical Character Recognition (OCR): OCR technology converts images of printed or typed text into machine-readable format. Over time, OCR has evolved from handling simple modern fonts to coping with complex layouts, multiple column formats, and even degraded print quality. For genealogical research, OCR makes it possible to quickly search and analyze digitized newspapers, city directories, or typewritten family histories.

Handwriting Recognition: While OCR excels at printed text, handwriting recognition is a more advanced task. Modern AI models, trained on tens of thousands of historical and modern handwriting samples, can interpret cursive letters, inconsistent letterforms, and unusual abbreviations. This technology is crucial for transcribing diaries, letters, parish registers, and other handwritten records that genealogists rely on.

Types of Documents Commonly Transcribed

- **Newspaper Articles and Obituaries:** Historical newspapers are treasure troves of genealogical data—local news, birth and death announcements, marriage notices, and social columns can reveal personal details about ancestors. After using OCR, you can transform these clippings into text that is easily searchable and can be summarized or analyzed using AI tools.

- **Vital Records (Birth, Marriage, Death Certificates):** Vital records often present a mix of printed headings and handwritten entries. OCR can handle the standardized printed parts, while specialized handwriting recognition tools (like Transkribus) interpret handwritten names, dates, and places. Once transcribed, these records can be incorporated into your genealogical database, making it simpler to connect individuals and trace lineages.

- **Census Records and Immigration Forms:** Census documents and passenger lists are often filled out by various clerks with varying handwriting styles. Handwriting recognition can help convert these complex tabular documents into structured text. With the resulting transcription, you can easily search for family members or analyze demographic trends.

- **Personal Letters, Diaries, and Family Correspondence:** These sources are highly valuable but often the most challenging to decipher. AI-powered transcription can handle much of the legwork, allowing you to focus on interpreting the meaning of the text, the relationships mentioned, and the social or emotional context revealed in private writings.

The Transcription Workflow

- **Digitize Your Source:** Start by creating high-quality digital images or scans of the documents. Aim for a high-resolution format (e.g., 300 dpi or higher) and ensure the image is as clear, well-lit, and straight as possible. Correct skewed pages and remove backgrounds or stains if you can, as clear inputs yield better transcription results.

- **Choose the Appropriate Tool**

  - **For Printed Text:** Basic OCR tools (Adobe Acrobat, Google Drive's OCR, ABBYY FineReader) handle modern or clearly printed documents well.

  - **For Historical Handwriting:** Specialized tools like Transkribus, which allows you to train custom models based on a sample set of documents, will yield superior results over generic OCR tools.

- For Complex Mixed Documents: A multi-step approach may be best—use one tool for printed headers and another for handwriting recognition. Some advanced AI platforms are now combining these steps.

- **Pre-Processing the Image:** Improve image quality by adjusting contrast, brightness, and orientation. Remove any extraneous borders or watermarks that might confuse the OCR engine. For handwriting, ensure that the text lines are as straight and isolated as possible.

- **Run the Transcription:** Upload your images to the chosen platform and run the transcription. For large volumes, consider batching the process. Many tools allow you to review transcribed text side-by-side with the original image, making it easier to identify errors.

- **Post-Processing and Correction:** Even the most advanced AI model will make mistakes. Review the resulting transcription for accuracy, focusing on surnames, place names, and old-fashioned terms. Correct errors directly in the tool if it allows, or in your preferred text editor afterward. This iterative correction process not only improves the current transcript but can, in some systems, train the model to perform better on future documents.

Strategies for Improving Transcription Accuracy

- **Train Custom Models:** If you have a large collection of documents with similar handwriting or formatting, consider training a custom model. For example, if you are consistently working with 19th-century German parish registers, feeding a tool like Transkribus sample transcriptions can dramatically enhance accuracy for that particular handwriting style or record format over time.

- **Contextual Clues:** Providing context can help language models interpret ambiguous words. For example, if you know the document is from a particular town, specify that so the tool can recognize place names more easily. Combine OCR output with a summarization tool like ChatGPT or Claude, providing historical context to improve the interpretation of unclear words.

- **Segmenting the Document:** Break large, complex documents into smaller segments—one page at a time or even one column at a time. Transcribing a manageable portion reduces the chance that the AI model will be overwhelmed by complexity and may result in fewer errors.

- **Iterative Validation:** Transcribe a few sample pages first, correct them thoroughly, and then use that corrected text to guide future transcriptions. By correcting errors early, you help refine the AI's internal understanding of the document's quirks.

Integrating Transcribed Text into Your Research

- **Searchability and Indexing:** Once you have a machine-readable transcription, you can search it instantly for family names, places, occupations, or events. This capability transforms historical documents from static images into dynamic research data, accelerating the discovery of relevant information.

- **Data Extraction and Analysis:** Clean transcribed text can be imported into genealogy databases or spreadsheets. You can then use tools like Excel or specialized genealogy software to sort, filter, and analyze data. For example, you might track the migration patterns of a family over several censuses or compare marriage records over multiple decades to understand changing family alliances.

- **Translation and Summarization:** After transcription, you can easily apply translation tools to foreign-language documents. Once translated, summarization models can highlight key events or list mentions of specific surnames. This layered approach—transcription, then translation, then summarization—enables non-native speakers to glean meaningful insights from ancestral records written in unfamiliar languages.

Challenges and Limitations

- **Degraded Documents:** Some historical documents are so faded, torn, or stained that even the best AI tools struggle. In these cases, manual transcription or consultation with a conservator or historian may still be necessary.

- **Archaic Scripts and Languages:** Medieval scripts, heavily stylized calligraphy, or shorthand notations present unique difficulties. While AI tools are improving, they may require substantial custom training or expert guidance. Sometimes, combining an AI-generated draft with a historian's or experienced researcher's knowledge is the best solution.

- **Accuracy vs. Speed:** While AI greatly speeds initial transcription, genealogists should remain vigilant. Automated transcription is a starting point, not a final result. Always verify and correct the text, especially if you plan to rely on it for critical genealogical conclusions.

Practical Examples

Example 1: Transcribing a Newspaper Death Notice dated 1924 in JPG format.

- Scan the newspaper clipping and save as JPG image.

- Upload the image to ChatGPT.

- Use prompt ***transcribe exactly including line breaks as shown in image***

- Proof and check generative text for errors.

Notes and test results can be found in **Appendix 4 – Transcribing Practical Example 1 –** *Drowned at Long Beach*.

Example 2: Transcribing a Baptism Certificate Form completed with handwritten text dated 1958 in JPG format

- The certificate was scanned and saved as JPG image.

- The JPG was uploaded to ChatGPT.

- ChatGPT versions used included 4 (free) and 4o (paid).

- Prompt: ***transcribe exactly***.

Notes and test results can be found in **Appendix 5 –** *Transcribing Practical Example 2 – Certificate of Baptism of Barbara Jacqueline Austin*.

Example 3: Transcribing a handwritten affidavit dated 1819 in JPG format

- The letter was downloaded from the National Archives and Records Administration and saved as JPG image.

- The JPG was uploaded to ChatGPT.

- ChatGPT versions used included 4 (free) and 4o (paid).

- Prompt: *transcribe exactly this handwritten affidavit of Ebenezer Horsam dated 17 July 1819 as part of a US Revolutionary War Pension file*.

Notes and test results can be found in **Appendix 6 – Transcribing Practical Example 3 – Handwritten Affidavit of Ebenezer Horsam dated 1819**

Future Developments in Transcription Technology

As AI continues to evolve, we can expect improvements in:

- **Multilingual Handwriting Models:** More robust tools for scripts like Cyrillic, Gothic, or older forms of Latin script, enabling genealogists to handle diverse linguistic backgrounds.

- **Context-Aware Models:** Tools that factor in historical periods, regional naming conventions, or domain-specific dictionaries for more accurate transcription.

- **Integration with Archives:** Closer collaboration between archives, libraries, and AI developers may result in pre-trained models specifically designed for common record sets, reducing the learning curve for genealogists.

* * *

I've always said that transcription is like a front door key—it opens up a whole new world of understanding when it comes to our ancestors' records. Thanks to tools like AI-driven OCR and handwriting recognition, genealogists now have powerful ways to transform static document images into clean, searchable text that's ready for real research. The secret is in the prep work—take time to organize your materials, choose the right software, and keep refining your process. Doing so means cutting down on the legwork and letting the technology do the heavy lifting. Before you know it, those old newspapers, handwritten ledgers, and personal letters become true treasure troves, making it easier to drill down into your family's past and bring a more informed, data-driven approach to your genealogy.

Chapter 5: Translating Historical Documents

As you delve deeper into your family history, it's almost guaranteed you'll bump into documents that aren't in your native language. Our ancestors often crossed borders—both real and cultural—leaving behind a paper trail recorded in Latin from church registers, German in Austro-Hungarian civil documents, Italian parish books, Cyrillic-script manifests for Eastern European immigrants, or the kind of old-time English that reads more like a riddle than a record. Without a proper translation, these rich sources remain locked away, their hidden stories untold.

This is where artificial intelligence can lend a much-needed helping hand. Today's translation tools are more advanced than ever, and when you guide them with the right context and historical insight, they can break down those language barriers and give you the keys to your ancestors' lives. But keep in mind—old documents don't always play by the rules. Obsolete terms, unusual spellings, unique handwriting styles, and local dialects can throw a wrench into the works of a generic translation engine.

That's why a thoughtful approach makes all the difference. By understanding the historical background of your sources, choosing the right tools, and following a tried-and-true workflow, you can turn mysterious scripts into meaningful stories. Armed with these strategies, you'll find that family records once lost in translation can now shine a light on the past, bringing your ancestors' voices back to life.

The Importance of Contextualizing Historical Documents

Time Period and Region

Language evolves over time. Terms that were common in the 17th century may no longer be in use, or their meanings may have shifted. Specifying the era and region of the document (e.g., "a German-language marriage record from 1870 in rural Austria") helps AI tools focus on historically appropriate vocabulary and spelling variants.

Document Type

Different types of documents use distinct language registers and terminologies. A birth certificate from early 20th-century Italy may have standardized legal terminology, while a personal letter from the 18th century may feature colloquialisms or family-specific nicknames. Identifying the nature of the document—church record, civil register, probate record, personal letter—guides the AI to expect certain patterns and vocabulary sets.

Cultural and Religious Context

Religious documents, such as Latin baptismal or marriage entries, might include abbreviations and phrases derived from liturgical texts. Understanding the religious or cultural context encourages the AI to interpret terms according to their appropriate cultural and historical meanings.

Known Family Data

If you know that your ancestors lived in a particular village, had certain surnames, or were associated with certain professions, share these details upfront. For example: "I am translating a Polish marriage record from the late 19th century. The family's surname is Kowalski, and they lived in the Mazovia region." This information helps the AI correctly identify key personal and place names.

Combining OCR/HTR with Translation

Before translating, ensure the text is machine-readable. If the source is a handwritten letter or a faded parish record, start by using OCR or handwriting recognition (as discussed in Chapter 4). Once you have a digital text output, you can feed it into translation models.

Workflow Example

- **OCR/HTR Process:** Use Transkribus to transcribe a handwritten German church register entry.

- **Quality Check:** Verify and correct any transcription errors, ensuring names and places are spelled as accurately as possible.

- **Contextual Prompting:** Instruct the AI translator: "This is an 1870 marriage record from Lower Austria, written in German. Please translate it into English. The groom's surname is 'Müller' and the bride's surname is 'Schmidt.' Focus on accuracy of names, occupations, and any mentions of parental details."

- **Refine and Verify:** Check the translated text. If certain words seem off or archaic, ask the AI to clarify: "What does the term 'Leineweber' mean in this historical context?" The AI can explain that it means "linen weaver," a common occupation at the time.

Tools and Platforms for Translation

General AI Translators

- **ChatGPT or Claude:** These large language models can handle a variety of languages and can be guided with context. While not primarily designed as translators, their flexibility and reasoning abilities can sometimes outperform standalone machine translation tools for historical or niche terminology.

- **Google Translate:** Quick and convenient, Google Translate provides instant translation for numerous languages. It works best with modern text but can serve as a baseline. Providing context and verifying results with another tool or a historical dictionary is advised.

- **Microsoft Translator:** Similar to Google Translate, with extensive language coverage. Can integrate with Microsoft 365 Copilot in the future, streamlining translation tasks if your documents are stored in the Microsoft ecosystem.

Specialized Tools or Models

- **Custom Trained Models:** Some platforms allow you to train language models on specialized glossaries or sets of historical texts. This can be especially useful for documents in Latin, Old German (Kurrentschrift, Sütterlin), or other archaic scripts.

- **Human-AI Hybrid Approaches:** If an AI translation seems uncertain, consider consulting a human translator with expertise in historical documents. The AI translation provides a rough draft, and the expert can correct nuances and explain context. This hybrid approach is often the gold standard for complex translations.

Dealing with Archaic Language and Scripts

Archaic Terms and Spellings

Old documents often contain words not found in modern dictionaries. Provide the AI with instructions, such as:

> *"If you encounter words you do not recognize, suggest possible meanings or ask me for clarification. These documents date from the 1700s in rural Bavaria and may use archaic German terms."*

AI and Genealogy A Practical Guide to Summarizing, Transcribing, and Translating Historical Records

This might prompt the AI to offer alternate translations or explanations.

Obsolete Letterforms and Scripts

Some historical languages, such as old German handwriting (Kurrentschrift) or Gothic typefaces (Fraktur), complicate character recognition. After transcription, note that the original text used Fraktur or Kurrentschrift:

> *"The following text was originally written in Fraktur script, which often uses slightly different letterforms. The place names and family names are German. Please keep that in mind when translating."*

This helps the AI avoid confusing certain letters and offers more accurate translations.

Dealing with Latin Records

Many church records, especially Catholic parish registers, were kept in Latin. While simple Latin terms for baptisms, marriages, and deaths are consistent, more complex notes may require additional clarification. You could tell the AI:

> *"This Latin text is from an 18th-century Catholic parish register in Lombardy, Italy. Common words like 'baptizatus' (baptized) or 'filius' (son of) are expected. Please translate to English and retain the original Latin name forms."*

Quality Assurance in Translation

Cross-Verification with Dictionaries

Check unusual words against historical dictionaries, genealogical glossaries, or resources like FamilySearch Wiki, which often lists old genealogical terms. For instance, if the translation includes an occupation that seems unfamiliar, query the AI:

The AI might respond that "Förster" means "forester" or "gamekeeper," providing a critical clue about your ancestor's occupation.

Multiple Translation Tools

Run the text through two different translators. If differences arise, ask the AI to reconcile them or provide an explanation. By comparing outputs, you can identify which version seems more historically consistent or linguistically plausible.

Iterative Refinement

If the initial translation doesn't capture certain nuances, revise your prompt. Add more historical context, clarify family names and locations, or specify which details are most important. By refining your instructions, you often get a more accurate and context-rich final translation.

Translating Various Document Types

Legal Documents and Affidavits

Documents like wills, property deeds, or affidavits may use formal, legalistic language and standardized phrases. Providing this context helps the AI predict the tone and vocabulary. For example:

Correspondence and Diaries

Personal letters and diaries often include colloquial expressions, emotional tone, and unique nicknames. Make sure the AI knows it's a personal communication:

AI and Genealogy A Practical Guide to Summarizing, Transcribing, and Translating Historical Records

Affidavits and Immigration Papers

For immigration documents, explaining the nature of the text is crucial.

Building a Translation Glossary

Over time, genealogists often encounter recurring terms, place names, and abbreviations. Maintain a glossary of these words and their meanings. For instance, if you frequently research German documents, keep a list of common terms like "Hofbesitzer" (farm owner), "Knecht" (farmhand), or "Witwe" (widow). Include this glossary in your prompt to the AI:

This technique improves consistency and accuracy as you build up a personalized reference over multiple research sessions.

Practical Examples

Example 1: Translating a page from a late 19th century French book in JPG format into English.

- Scan the book page and save as JPG image.

- Upload the image to ChatGPT.

- Use prompt ***Translate this page from Le troisième centenaire de l'Édit de Nantes en Amérique et en France published 1898 from French to English***

- Proof and check generative text for errors.

Notes and test results can be found in **Appendix 7 – Translating Practical Example 1 – *Le troisième centenaire de l'Édit de Nantes en Amérique et en France***.

Example 2: Transcribing and Translating a German Parish Record in JPG format

- Scan the document and save it as JPG image.

- Transcribe the German text using ChatGPT with this prompt: ***transcribe exactly this German marriage record***.

- Check the transcribed text against the original.

- Copy the transcribed text and paste it into ChatGPT with this prompt: ***translate exactly this German text from a marriage record***.

- Check the translated text against the original.

Notes and test results can be found in **Appendix 8 – Translating Practical Example 2 – *German Marriage Record***.

Future Trends in AI Translation for Genealogy

As AI evolves, expect improved handling of archaic languages, dialects, and script forms. Future models may incorporate historical corpora, allowing them to more accurately translate texts from any era. Integration of genealogical data into AI training sets might even lead to tools that automatically detect and interpret family relationships, social standings, and occupational titles common in older records.

* * *

One of the most exciting aspects of today's genealogy landscape is the ability to tap into records written in languages you might never have studied. And let's face it—when you're trying to decode old documents, every bit of help matters. That's where AI steps in to lend a hand. Imagine pairing OCR and handwriting recognition with targeted prompts and a bit of trial-and-error to guide AI into producing translations you can actually work with. Sure, there are still hurdles—old-fashioned wording and quirky phrases can sometimes throw these tools off. But overall, they're breaking down language barriers and letting us see into corners of the past we used to leave unexplored. Over time, as you refine your process and gain confidence, you'll discover that AI-assisted translations become an indispensable tool in unlocking your ancestors' stories and adding new depth to your family history research.

Chapter 6: AI and Source Citations

If you're just getting started in genealogy, one of the first lessons you'll learn is how critical source citations are to proving family connections and verifying the details of an ancestor's life. In fact, citing your sources is about much more than just writing down where you found that birth date or marriage record. It's all about creating a roadmap so that others—now and in the future—can follow in your research footsteps. This includes everything from traditional record sets like census schedules and death certificates to personal items like old family letters and diaries.

Don't let the idea of citations intimidate you. Focus on four simple elements: **what** information you uncovered, **where** you discovered it, **how** you accessed it, and the **specific details** that would help another researcher find it again. By keeping things straightforward and consistent, you'll not only reinforce the credibility of your work, but also set the stage for a more collaborative family history journey.

For artificial intelligence content, here's the formula you might consider using as proposed by the Modern Language Association of America (MLA):

> "[QUERY]" prompt. [NAME OF AI PLATFORM], [DATE OR VERSION OF PLATFORM], [NAME OF AI COMPANY], [DATE OF QUERY], [PLATFORM URL]

So, if I asked ChatGPT to translate a page from the book *Le troisième centenaire de l'Édit de Nantes en Amérique et en France*, here is the source citation I would use:

> "Translate to English" prompt using digital image of *Le troisième centenaire de l'Édit de Nantes en Amérique et en France*, page 3, published 1989. ChatGPT, ChatGPT 4.o version, OpenAI, 12 November 2024, https://chat.openai.com/.

Chapter 7: Ethical, Privacy, and Accuracy Considerations in AI-Assisted Genealogical Research

As we move deeper into the digital age, it's no surprise that artificial intelligence is reshaping our genealogical research methods—whether it's summarizing old documents, transcribing hard-to-read records, or translating foreign-language materials. But let's face it: with these newfound capabilities come serious responsibilities.

In this chapter, I'll cut through the hype to show you how to use AI tools effectively while keeping ethics, privacy, and cultural sensitivities front and center. We'll also talk about how to confirm data accuracy and maintain the highest professional standards. By the end, you'll be equipped not only to harness the power of AI in your genealogy work, but to do so in a way that respects individuals, communities, and the integrity of our shared past.

Understanding the Sensitivity of Personal and Historical Data

Private vs. Public Records

Genealogical research often involves working with a blend of public and private documents. Census records, immigration manifests, and some civil registration documents may be widely available and fall under public domain or open-access rules. In contrast, personal letters, diaries, or family legal documents might contain sensitive information—details about family disputes, adoptions, health conditions, or religious affiliations—that descendants may wish to keep private.

Digital Vulnerabilities

Once documents are digitized and processed by AI tools, they can be easily shared, duplicated, and indexed. This convenience poses risks if personal or confidential information falls into the wrong hands or is used without appropriate consent. Researchers must consider the digital footprint they create when uploading documents to online platforms, including those powered by AI.

Ensuring Compliant Use of AI Tools and Data

Reading Terms of Service

Before uploading documents to AI platforms, genealogists should carefully review the terms of service and privacy policies. Some AI providers may store input data to improve their models, raising concerns about long-term data retention. Understanding how your chosen platform handles user-submitted data is crucial for maintaining privacy.

Opting for Secure Solutions

Where possible, select AI tools with robust data protection measures—end-to-end encryption, clear data deletion policies, and compliance with regulations such as the General Data Protection Regulation (GDPR) in Europe. Consider paid services that promise greater privacy or use on-premises or self-hosted AI solutions that allow you full control over your data.

Consent and Copyright

If you are working with documents that involve living individuals, ensure you have the necessary permissions to share or process their information. Similarly, verify that the documents you upload are not protected by copyright. Ethical genealogical practice means respecting intellectual property rights and the wishes of document owners.

Cultural and Historical Sensitivities

Contextual Awareness

Historical documents may reflect cultural norms, language, and attitudes that differ significantly from modern standards. Certain records might contain offensive terms, reflect

AI and Genealogy A Practical Guide to Summarizing, Transcribing, and Translating Historical Records

discrimination, or perpetuate historical injustices. When summarizing or translating these documents, AI might replicate these biases or fail to provide sensitive context.

Highlighting Sensitive Content

When working with AI, consider prompting it to note and contextualize sensitive or outdated language. For instance, instruct the model to:

> *"Identify any archaic or offensive terms in the following text and provide an explanatory note reflecting their historical context."*

Engaging with Community Guidelines

If you are sharing AI-processed documents with family members, local historians, or genealogical communities, present potentially sensitive material with care. Provide content warnings or explanatory notes to avoid causing offense or misunderstanding.

Accuracy and Verification Challenges

AI Hallucinations and Errors

AI tools, while powerful, are not infallible. They may produce "hallucinations"—fabricated details or misinterpretations. This risk is heightened when dealing with archaic languages, complex handwriting, or documents lacking clear context. Always treat AI output as a starting point, subject to human verification.

Establishing Quality Control Measures

- **Cross-Verification:** Compare the AI's transcription or translation against the original document. When summarizing, verify that key facts align with what you know from other reputable sources.

- **Iterative Refinement:** If the AI makes an error, correct it and re-run the process. Iterative improvements lead to better results over time.

- **Seeking Expert Input:** For critical documents or challenging translations, consult historians, archivists, or professional translators. A human expert can provide guidance that AI currently lacks, especially for complex or emotionally charged materials.

Documenting Your Process

Keep a record of which tools and prompts you used, as well as any corrections made. This audit trail ensures that future researchers can understand your methodology and trust the integrity of your findings.

Ethical Considerations in Presentation and Publication

Responsible Sharing of Family Histories

Genealogy is often a family affair, and the stories you uncover may have repercussions for living relatives. Before publishing AI-generated transcripts or translations, consider the potential impact on privacy, family relationships, and personal sensitivities.

Balancing Transparency and Discretion

While genealogists value accuracy and completeness, not every fact must be broadcast publicly. If you discover sensitive information—such as details of a secret adoption or an ancestor's criminal record—consider whether it should be shared widely. Ethically, maintaining respect for the privacy and dignity of living relatives often takes precedence over public disclosure.

Citing AI Outputs Properly

If you rely on AI-generated translations or summaries, note this in your genealogical citations. Transparency about your research methods builds trust and helps other researchers understand how you arrived at your conclusions.

AI and Genealogy A Practical Guide to Summarizing, Transcribing, and Translating Historical Records

The Evolving Landscape of AI Ethics

Anticipating Regulatory Changes

Laws and regulations governing data privacy and AI use are rapidly evolving. Keep an eye on developments at the regional, national, and international levels. Familiarize yourself with professional genealogical standards and guidelines that address AI usage, and adapt your practices as standards evolve.

Promoting Best Practices in the Genealogical Community

Discuss ethical and privacy considerations with fellow genealogists. Share your experiences, lessons learned, and strategies for respectful, privacy-aware research. By collectively setting high standards, the genealogical community can ensure that AI serves as a force for good, enhancing our understanding of the past without compromising personal or cultural integrity.

* * *

In today's AI-driven genealogy landscape, keeping ethical, privacy, and accuracy issues front and center is more than just good practice—it's essential. By taking time to understand the risks, establish sound guidelines, and follow a clear code of conduct, we can use these cutting-edge tools to uncover our ancestors' stories with integrity. Treating personal data, cultural traditions, and individual narratives with care not only honors the past but also supports the trust and respect that bind our genealogical community together. As AI continues to evolve, staying informed, aware, and ethically committed ensures that family history research remains both illuminating and humane.

Chapter 8: Tips and Tricks for Summarizing, Transcribing, and Translating Genealogy Documents

Imagine you're knee-deep in old documents, ready to squeeze every last drop of data from them. The key to getting the most out of today's AI tools is simple: combine a thoughtful strategy with clear, guided instructions. Of course, each record has its own quirks, so don't expect a one-size-fits-all solution. Still, the tips and tactics I've gathered here are designed to help you sharpen your workflows, improve accuracy, and shave precious time off those tasks—whether you're summarizing, transcribing, or translating the genealogical treasures you've uncovered.

General Strategies for Working with AI Tools

Combine Multiple Tools

Rather than relying on one platform for all tasks, leverage each tool's specialty. For example, use Transkribus for transcription, ChatGPT for summarization, and Google Translate for initial translations. Then, compare and refine the results.

Iterative Improvement

AI output improves when you refine prompts and re-run tasks. If the first summary or translation is vague, provide additional context or correct misunderstandings and ask the model to try again.

Keep a Research Log

Document which prompts, tools, and settings yield the best results. Over time, you'll develop a personalized "playbook" that streamlines your process and enhances accuracy.

Verify Against Known Facts

Always cross-check AI-generated outputs with known family data, historical facts, or other reliable sources. AI should complement, not replace, your critical analysis and historical knowledge.

Context, Context, Context

The more historical and cultural context you provide (e.g., specifying the time period, region, language nuances, and known family details), the better the AI will perform in summarizing, transcribing, and translating documents.

Tips for Summarizing Genealogy Documents

Focus Your Prompt

Instead of a generic "summarize this document," specify what you're looking for:

> *"Summarize key events related to the Wilson family migration from Ireland to Canada in the 1850s found in these 50 pages."*

Break Documents into Manageable Chunks

If dealing with a very large text, summarize it chapter by chapter or section by section. Then, ask the AI to create a master summary from these partial summaries.

Highlight Important Terms

Before summarizing, tell the AI which surnames, places, or events matter to you. This ensures the summary highlights relevant details rather than generic information.

Ask for Different Levels of Detail

Start with a high-level overview. If something seems interesting—such as a particular family's migration—request a more granular summary focusing only on that topic.

Use Summaries as a Discovery Tool

Summaries can help identify which sections of a long text contain valuable genealogical details, saving you from reading irrelevant pages. Once you know where the "golden nuggets" are, you can do a closer reading or a more detailed analysis.

Tips for Transcribing Historical Documents

High-Quality Images

Crisp, well-lit scans lead to better OCR and handwriting recognition. Make sure your documents are scanned at a high resolution (300 dpi or more) and are properly aligned and cropped.

Use Specialized Tools for Handwriting

For handwritten letters, diaries, or parish registers, a dedicated tool like Transkribus can significantly outperform generic OCR. Invest the time to learn such tools for better results.

Train Custom Models if Possible

If you have many similar documents (e.g., the same clerk's handwriting in multiple census records), training a custom model on a subset of your data can dramatically improve accuracy in future transcriptions.

Edit and Correct Early and Often

After the first transcription pass, review and correct errors immediately. This "teaches" some AI tools to improve on subsequent pages and also prevents the spread of inaccuracies through your research notes.

Leverage Historical Dictionaries and Reference Works

When faced with unclear words, check contemporary dictionaries or historical glossaries. Providing the AI with the meaning of unusual terms can improve future transcriptions and translations.

Segment the Document

If a document is complex (multiple columns, marginal notes), break it into segments and transcribe each segment separately. This approach reduces confusion and improves accuracy.

Tips for Translating Genealogy Documents

Always Provide Context
Specify the type of document (birth certificate, church register, immigration manifest), the date range, the region, and the language. Inform the AI if the text is archaic or uses outdated spelling.

Identify Proper Nouns
Alert the AI to known family names, place names, and occupations. For example:

> *"The surname Müller is significant. Please retain it as a surname and do not translate it."*

Check Against Historical Resources
Compare unusual translations with historical dictionaries, genealogical forums, or language-specific guides found on FamilySearch Wiki or Cyndi's List.

Refine Prompts for Better Accuracy
If the initial translation is literal or misses nuance, ask for a more culturally informed version or request that the model explain archaic terms.

> *"Please clarify the term 'Stallknecht' in this 18th-century German context."*

Maintain a Translation Glossary
Keep track of recurring words, titles, professions, and religious or legal terms. Include this glossary in future prompts to improve translation consistency and accuracy.

Use Multiple Translation Tools

For complex or sensitive translations, compare outputs from different AI translators and consult a human expert if necessary. The goal is not just a literal translation but an accurate, context-rich understanding of the text.

Combining Summarization, Transcription, and Translation

Workflow Order Matters

Typically, you'll first transcribe a document (if it's an image) before summarizing or translating. Once you have a clean, searchable text, you can easily apply translation or summarization without redoing steps.

Summarize Before Translating Lengthy Texts

If a document is long and entirely in a foreign language, consider summarizing it first to determine if it's relevant. If so, translate only the important sections.

Contextualize Before Each New Step

Remind the AI about the nature of the document and any relevant historical background before asking for summaries or translations. Carry context from the transcription phase forward into the translation phase.

Record Your Process

Keep notes on each step—transcription accuracy, specific terms, what worked well—so that when you return to a similar document later, you can replicate and refine your successful methods.

Final Considerations

Set Realistic Expectations

AI tools greatly speed up certain tasks, but they are not infallible. Expect some errors, and treat AI output as a starting point.

Use AI as a Research Assistant, Not a Replacement

While these tools can handle repetitive tasks and grunt work, human expertise remains essential. Your understanding of historical context, your ability to spot inconsistencies, and your critical thinking are irreplaceable.

Practice Makes Perfect

The more you work with these tools, the better you'll become at crafting effective prompts, fine-tuning results, and integrating AI outputs into your research workflow.

* * *

When you embrace these tips and tricks, you're not just tapping into the power of AI—you're taking a big step forward in your family history journey. Starting with good scanning habits, using well-crafted prompts, verifying results, and setting up a workflow tailored to your needs, you'll quickly see improvements in your research. As you develop your own toolkit, AI-assisted summarization, transcription, and translation become essential partners in tracking down those elusive ancestors and breaking through longstanding brick walls. Before you know it, you'll be uncovering new family stories at a faster pace and with greater confidence.

Chapter 9: Resources for Genealogy Document Processing

Glossary

- **Abstractive Summarization:** A technique in AI that generates a concise version of text using new phrasing rather than directly quoting the original. This approach captures the main ideas in a human-like summary.

- **AI (Artificial Intelligence):** A field of computer science focused on creating systems that can perform tasks that typically require human intelligence. In genealogy, AI can assist with summarizing long texts, transcribing documents, and translating foreign-language records.

- **API (Application Programming Interface):** A set of tools and protocols allowing different software systems to interact. Some AI tools can be integrated into genealogical workflows via their APIs, enabling custom automation and data processing.

- **Archaic Language:** Old or outdated forms of language that may appear in historical documents. AI tools may need historical and contextual details to accurately interpret and translate archaic words or phrases.

- **ChatGPT (OpenAI):** A large language model capable of understanding and generating text. Used by genealogists for summarizing documents, providing initial translations, and clarifying historical context.

- **Claude (Anthropic):** Another advanced language model known for handling long text inputs and maintaining coherent dialogue, useful for large genealogical documents or complex historical narratives.

- **Contextual Prompting:** Providing background information—such as time period, location, and document type—to guide an AI model. Contextual details improve the quality of summaries, transcriptions, and translations.

- **Copilot / Microsoft 365 Copilot:** AI assistants initially developed for coding or productivity tasks but adaptable to genealogical workflows. They can help with text-related tasks, workflow automation, and document analysis.

- **Cultural Sensitivities:** Aspects of historical documents that reflect outdated attitudes, offensive terms, or sensitive cultural and religious content. Genealogists and AI tools must approach these details ethically and with proper context.

- **Data Privacy and Security:** Concerns about how digitized genealogical documents and personal family data are stored, processed, and shared. Ensuring the confidentiality and ethical use of data is essential when using AI tools.

- **Digitization:** The process of converting physical documents (letters, certificates, newspapers) into digital images or text. A necessary first step before applying OCR, summarization, or translation tools.

- **Extractive Summarization:** A method of summarization that selects key sentences or paragraphs from the original text without rewriting them. Useful for quickly identifying important sections but may be less coherent than abstractive methods.

- **Handwriting Recognition (HTR):** A specialized form of OCR designed to read handwritten text. Essential for genealogical documents like diaries, letters, and old parish registers that are not machine printed.

- **Historical Context:** Information about the time period, location, culture, and social conditions under which a document was created. Providing historical context to AI models improves accuracy in summarizing, transcribing, and translating.

- **Hallucinations:** Errors generated by AI models where they produce fabricated facts or details not found in the original text. These inaccuracies highlight the importance of verifying AI outputs.

- **Large Language Models (LLMs):** Advanced AI systems trained on vast amounts of text. LLMs like GPT-4 and Claude can summarize documents, answer questions, and assist with translations when properly guided.

- **Machine Translation (MT):** AI-driven translation of text from one language to another. Useful for genealogists who encounter documents in foreign languages, but often requires contextual cues for accuracy.

- **Metadata:** Information describing a document (e.g., date, author, region). Including metadata in AI prompts improves the model's understanding and boosts transcription or translation quality.

- **OCR (Optical Character Recognition):** Technology that converts scanned images of printed or typed documents into machine-readable text. It's the first step in making historical records searchable and analyzable by AI tools.

- **Perplexity AI:** A research-oriented AI assistant that provides concise answers with citations. Can help genealogists verify historical facts, identify reputable sources, and contextualize documents.

- **Privacy Policies and Terms of Service:** Legal and ethical guidelines provided by AI tools and platforms. Reviewing these helps ensure data handling aligns with genealogical researchers' privacy and security needs.

- **Prompt Engineering:** Crafting instructions and background details for AI tools. Thoughtful prompting guides AI toward more accurate and relevant outputs, especially in genealogical tasks involving complex historical contexts.

- **Summarization:** The process of condensing long documents into shorter, more manageable overviews that highlight key points, individuals, dates, and places relevant to genealogical research.

- **Transcription:** The act of converting handwritten or printed text from documents into machine-readable, searchable text. Transcription often involves OCR or handwriting recognition, especially for older sources.

- **Transkribus:** A platform specializing in the transcription of historical handwritten documents. It uses AI to improve accuracy over time, particularly useful for diaries, letters, and registers that are challenging to decode.

- **Verification:** The process of checking AI-generated outputs against the original documents, known historical facts, or additional resources. Verification ensures accuracy and maintains genealogical research standards.

- **Vital Records:** Official documents recording life events such as births, marriages, and deaths. Vital records often combine printed forms with handwritten entries, requiring both OCR and handwriting recognition to fully digitize.

- **Workflows:** The structured processes genealogists create, combining multiple AI tools and steps (e.g., digitization → OCR → translation → summarization → verification) to efficiently handle large volumes of historical data.

AI Platforms

- **ChatGPT:** https://openai.com
- **Claude:** https://anthropic.com
- **Copilot:** https://copilot.microsoft.com/
- **Gemini:** https://gemini.google.com/
- **Perplexity:** https://www.perplexity.ai/

AI Tools

- **FamilySearch Labs Full Text Indexing:** https://www.familysearch.org/search/full-text
- **Summarize! ChatGPT:** https://chat.openai.com/g/g-Lj07Aq7sC-summarize
- **Transkribus:** https://readcoop.eu/transkribus

AI and Genealogy Communities

- **AI Genealogy Insights** – Blog https://aigenealogyinsights.com/author/digitalarchivst/
- **Genealogy and Artificial Intelligence (AI) -** Facebook group https://www.facebook.com/groups/1255245945084761

Articles and Videos:

- ***10 ChatGPT Prompts Every Genealogist Needs to Know*** - Findmypast YouTube channel https://www.youtube.com/live/EbRXzd2SmNM
- ***AI & Genealogy: Harnessing the Power of Artificial Intelligence for Family History Research*** – MyHeritage Knowledgebase https://education.myheritage.com/article/ai-

genealogy-harnessing-the-power-of-artificial-intelligence-for-family-history-research/

- ***AI Developments in Genealogy*** – FamilySearch
  https://www.familysearch.org/en/blog/ai-developments-genealogy

- ***AI Revolutionizes Genealogy: Discovering Family History and Relationships with Data-Driven Insights*** – LinkedIn
  https://www.linkedin.com/pulse/ai-revolutionizes-genealogy-discovering-family-history-pillai/

- ***A Genealogist's Guide to Artificial Intelligence*** – Family Tree Magazine
  https://familytreemagazine.com/resources/software/ai-and-genealogy/

- ***Genealogy Meets AI: Expert Guide to ChatGPT, Claude, and Beyond*** – Genealogy with Dana Leeds YouTube channel
  https://youtu.be/5jT2KYepyCk

- ***How to use AI in genealogical research*** – MyHeritage Wiki
  https://www.myheritage.com/wiki/How_to_use_AI_in_genealogical_research

- ***How to use AI to translate birth, marriage and death records, books, notes on photos and much more*** – Italian Roots and Genealogy YouTube channel
  https://www.youtube.com/live/_gxKE-d8OPs

- **RootsTech AI Videos** – FamilySearch
  https://www.familysearch.org/en/rootstech/search?f.language=en-US&f.text=AI&p.index=0

- ***Success at Transcribing Russian Handwriting with AI!*** – BEHOLD Genealogy
  https://www.beholdgenealogy.com/blog/?p=3917

- ***The Strategy of Using AI for Genealogical Research*** – BYU Library Family History YouTube channel
  https://youtu.be/vixlWg31nFg

- ***Top Ten AI Genealogy Breakthroughs of 2024*** – AI Genealogy Insights
  https://aigenealogyinsights.com/2024/11/19/top-ten-ai-genealogy-breakthroughs-of-2024/

- ***Using AI to translate and transcribe genealogy documents*** – MyHeritage Wiki
  https://www.myheritage.com/wiki/Using_AI_to_translate_and_transcribe_genealogy_documents

AI and Genealogy A Practical Guide to Summarizing, Transcribing, and Translating Historical Records

Appendix 1: Translating Jewish Records in Cyrillic, Hebrew, and Yiddish Printed Text and Handwriting

Below is a guide to employing modern AI platforms to translate Jewish genealogy records from Cyrillic, Hebrew, and Yiddish sources. These methods encompass both printed and handwritten materials, reflecting the complexity of historical documents and the interdisciplinary expertise required. The topics discussed include capabilities, workflows, best practices, and examples for major AI tools such as ChatGPT, Claude, Microsoft's Copilot (web-version), Google's Gemini (expected), Perplexity, and Transkribus.

Understanding the Historical Context and Linguistic Challenges

Jewish genealogy records—birth certificates, marriage contracts (ketubot), death notices, community registers, and immigration lists—often appear in multiple scripts and languages, reflecting the fluidity of Jewish communities across Eastern Europe and the Middle East. Translators must contend with:

- **Cyrillic:** Common in Russian Empire-era vital records, 19th–20th century Poland, Ukraine, Lithuania, and Belarus. Historical Cyrillic script and archaic orthographic conventions can challenge modern OCR (Optical Character Recognition) and translation systems.

- **Hebrew:** Found in religious records, community minutes, rabbinical correspondence, and old synagogue registers. The vowel-pointing (niqqud) often is omitted, and cursive or Rashi script variations appear frequently.

- **Yiddish:** Predominantly written in the Hebrew alphabet, Yiddish materials can vary widely in orthography and style. Early 20th-century European records or old newspapers can contain unique spellings and handwriting.

For accurate translation, one often needs to combine specialized OCR solutions with powerful Large Language Models (LLMs) or multi-modal AI platforms.

Platforms and Their Roles

Transkribus (OCR and Handwritten Text Recognition)

Primary Function: Transkribus is a leading platform for historical document analysis and transcription. It specializes in Handwritten Text Recognition (HTR) and OCR with custom models trained on historical scripts. For Jewish genealogy:

- **Cyrillic Documents:** Transkribus can process old print forms of Cyrillic with available model sets. For handwritten documents, custom training on sample pages may be necessary.

- **Hebrew and Yiddish:** While general OCR solutions may struggle, Transkribus offers models or can be trained on these scripts. The platform's community-driven model repository may contain pretrained models for Yiddish newspapers or Hebrew manuscripts.

Workflow:

- **Upload Scanned Documents:** Digitize your records at a high resolution (300 dpi or more) in TIFF or JPEG format.

- **Apply Script-Specific Models:** Choose or train a model optimized for historical Cyrillic, Hebrew, or Yiddish.

- **Export the Text:** Once recognition is complete, export text files (TXT, XML).

AI and Genealogy A Practical Guide to Summarizing, Transcribing, and Translating Historical Records

Practical Example:

Suppose you have a 19th-century Jewish birth register from Vitebsk (in today's Belarus) written in Cyrillic. Upload the scanned pages to Transkribus, apply a Cyrillic model optimized for historical documents, and then export the recognized text. You now have a workable digital transcription ready for translation.

ChatGPT (OpenAI) and Claude (Anthropic)

Primary Function: Both ChatGPT and Claude are Large Language Models capable of translating text directly. Their strengths lie in understanding context, even with less-than-perfect source text.

Use Case:

- After extracting text from Transkribus, you can input the Cyrillic, Hebrew, or Yiddish text into ChatGPT or Claude and request a direct translation into English.

- These models can handle slight orthographic variations, providing context-aware translations.

Workflow:

- **Prepare the OCR Text:** Ensure the text is as clean as possible (no stray OCR errors).

- **Prompt the LLM:** For example: "Please translate the following Yiddish text into English. The text is from a 1920s community record." Paste the text following the prompt.

- **Review and Edit:** Check the LLM's output and, if necessary, follow up with clarifying queries, such as "Can you verify the meaning of this term?" or "Does this name correspond to a known place?"

Practical Example:

- After using Transkribus on a page of a Yiddish death register from Warsaw (1910), you get a paragraph of Yiddish text. In ChatGPT, you type:

  User: "Translate the following Yiddish text into English: [pasted text]."

  ChatGPT: Returns a coherent translation, possibly with explanations of archaic terms.

Copilot (Microsoft Web-Version)

Primary Function: Microsoft's Copilot integrates Azure Cognitive Services (including vision and language models) and can assist in OCR and translation within the Microsoft ecosystem.

Use Case:

- For printed Cyrillic or Hebrew, you can upload a scanned document to Microsoft OneDrive or SharePoint, use Azure Cognitive OCR to extract text, and then leverage Copilot (or Microsoft Translator) for translation.

- For handwritten text, Copilot might suggest using a specialized Azure OCR endpoint first. Copilot can assist in streamlining the workflow by providing inline suggestions within Microsoft 365 apps (Word, Excel, PowerPoint) after you have transcribed the content.

Workflow:

- **OCR via Azure Cognitive Services:** Convert scanned images of Cyrillic or Hebrew records.

- **Integrate with Copilot:** In Word, open a blank document, copy the extracted text, and ask Copilot: "Please translate this Hebrew birth record into

English, maintaining the original names and place names."

- **Refine Output:** Adjust formatting or request clarifications from Copilot.

Practical Example:

- You have a printed Hebrew birth certificate from the 1930s. You run it through Azure OCR, then open Word with Copilot enabled:

  User: "Copilot, translate this Hebrew text into English: [paste text]."

  Copilot: Provides a line-by-line translation, including personal names and addresses.

Gemini (Google's Next-Generation Model, Anticipated Capabilities)

Primary Function: While not fully public at the time of writing, Google's Gemini is expected to combine the strengths of large language models with advanced multimodal capabilities.

Use Case:

- Gemini could potentially handle OCR and translation in a single step, especially given Google's strong background in language translation (Google Translate) and OCR (Document AI).

- For Jewish genealogical documents, Gemini might identify the script (Cyrillic, Hebrew, Yiddish), transcribe it, and translate it in one unified workflow.

Practical Example (Anticipated):

- You upload a photograph of a Yiddish newspaper obituary from 1915 into a Google Workspace integrated with Gemini.

User: "Gemini, transcribe and translate this Yiddish obituary into English."

Gemini: Automatically recognizes the script, performs OCR, then translates the text, possibly providing historical context or definitions of archaic terms.

Perplexity

Primary Function: Perplexity is a research assistant AI platform known for sourcing factual information and providing context from multiple documents.

Use Case:

- While not primarily an OCR tool, Perplexity can help you understand unusual historical terms encountered in the translated text. If you feed it context or a snippet of already-translated text, it can help clarify historical references, place names, or genealogical terms.

- Combine it with another tool like Transkribus for OCR and ChatGPT for translation, then turn to Perplexity for explanatory notes.

Practical Example:

- After translation, you find a place name unfamiliar to you: "Jurbarkas" mentioned in the Yiddish record.

  User: "Perplexity, what is Jurbarkas and what was its Jewish community like historically?"

  Perplexity: Provides a synthesized historical overview, aiding in genealogical research.

Best Practices

- **Combine OCR and LLMs:** Use specialized OCR (Transkribus or Azure OCR) to convert historical documents into editable text, then use LLMs (ChatGPT, Claude, Copilot) for translation.

- **Iterative Refinement:** After initial translation, clarify ambiguous terms.

- **Script-Specific Models:** For better accuracy, train or choose models known to handle historical Hebrew or Yiddish handwriting.

- **Contextual Prompts:** Provide context to the LLM— mention the date, region, type of document, and nature of the text to improve translation accuracy.

- **Proofreading and Verification:** Cross-check important facts (names, dates, places) against known genealogical databases or reference works. AI-generated translations are strong starting points but require human oversight.

Putting It All Together: A Step-by-Step Example

Scenario: You have a handwritten Yiddish birth registry entry from 1905 in Vilnius (Wilno).

- **Digitize and OCR:** Scan the document at high resolution and upload it to Transkribus. Select a pre-trained Yiddish HTR model and run the transcription.

- **Extract and Translate:** Copy the resulting Yiddish text and paste it into ChatGPT with a prompt: "Translate the following Yiddish birth entry from 1905 Vilnius into English. The entry may contain names of individuals and places. Preserve all personal names accurately."

- **Refine and Understand:** Once translated, if a place name or title is unclear, copy that snippet into Perplexity: "Provide historical context for the term

'Kehilla' as used in early 20th-century Lithuanian Jewish records."

- **Finalize:** Incorporate the refined translation, explanatory notes, and any corrections into your genealogical database or research notes.

* * *

By leveraging a combination of specialized OCR/HTR software (Transkribus), advanced LLMs (ChatGPT, Claude), integrated productivity AI (Copilot), forthcoming multimodal models (Gemini), and research assistants (Perplexity), genealogists can efficiently navigate and translate the complex linguistic landscape of Jewish historical records. The key lies in careful tool selection, iterative refining, and contextual knowledge, ensuring the most accurate and meaningful translations possible.

Appendix 2: Translating Records in German Fraktur Printed Text and Handwriting

When dealing with historical German genealogy records, researchers frequently encounter texts printed or handwritten in Fraktur—a Gothic script widely used in Germany until the mid-20th century. These documents often pose significant challenges even for fluent German speakers due to the unfamiliar letterforms and archaic vocabulary. Modern artificial intelligence (AI) tools, however, can greatly facilitate transcription and translation, streamlining the research process. The following guidance outlines how to leverage major AI platforms—such as OpenAI's ChatGPT, Anthropic's Claude, GitHub Copilot for the web, Google's Gemini (projected capabilities), Perplexity AI, and the Transkribus platform—to effectively translate German Fraktur records into modern German and English.

General Considerations for Using AI on Fraktur Texts

Before diving into specific platforms, it's crucial to recognize a few best practices:

- **High-Quality Images:** Ensure your source material is as clear as possible. High-resolution scans or photographs with good lighting and contrast will improve OCR (Optical Character Recognition) accuracy.

- **Preprocessing:** For printed Fraktur texts, automated OCR tools trained on Gothic fonts can yield very accurate transcriptions. Handwritten Fraktur may require specialized handwriting models, which Transkribus excels at providing.

- **Iterative Approach:** Start by obtaining a raw transcription from a handwriting recognition (HWR) or

OCR model and then use a large language model (LLM) to clarify archaic terms, standardize spelling, and produce translations.

- **Contextual Clarifications:** Supply LLMs with relevant context, such as historical periods, regional dialects, or genealogical terminology, to improve the accuracy and usefulness of translations.

Using ChatGPT (OpenAI) for Translation and Contextual Understanding

Functionality: ChatGPT can assist once you have a machine-readable transcription. If you already used Transkribus to convert your Fraktur scans into text, you can paste that text into ChatGPT for translation into modern German or English.

Practical Example:

- **User Input to ChatGPT:**

  "Below is a transcription of a birth record from 1885 in Fraktur. Please translate it into English and explain any archaic terms:

  'Geboren am 3ten März 1885, Johann Schmidt, Sohn des Bauers Heinrich Schmidt und seiner Ehefrau Maria geb. Müller…'"

- Expected ChatGPT Response:

  The model would translate: "Born on the 3rd of March 1885, Johann Schmidt, son of the farmer Heinrich Schmidt and his wife Maria née Müller…" and might add: "The term 'Bauer' at the time often indicated a farmer who owned land rather than just a hired farmhand."

Using Claude (Anthropic) for Deep Explanation and Disambiguation

Functionality: Claude, similar to ChatGPT, can provide translations and context, often excelling at more nuanced explanations due to its training data. Once you have your OCR or HWR transcription, you can prompt Claude to clarify unusual terms, obsolete spellings, or old-fashioned occupations, which are common in genealogical records.

Practical Example:

- **User Input to Claude:**

  "Please translate the following German Fraktur funeral announcement from 1910 into English and describe the meaning of 'Ackerknecht' in a historical German context:

  'Am 15ten Januar 1910 verschied unser geliebter Vater, der Ackerknecht Wilhelm Braun...'"

- **Expected Claude Response:**

  Claude would produce a translation: "On January 15, 1910, our beloved father, the farmhand (Ackerknecht) Wilhelm Braun, passed away..." and explain that "Ackerknecht" historically referred to a farm laborer who worked the fields, often hired seasonally or employed permanently by a landowner.

Using Copilot Microsoft Web-Version to Aid in OCR Script Handling

Functionality: While GitHub Copilot is primarily designed to assist in coding tasks, the web-based Copilot integration (such as in GitHub Codespaces or Visual Studio Code Web) can assist in building scripts that use OCR APIs, such as Tesseract OCR with Fraktur-trained models, or calling external OCR services. Copilot can suggest code snippets to automate image preprocessing, batch OCR conversions, and subsequent translation calls to APIs.

Practical Example (Workflow):

- In VS Code Web with Copilot enabled, type a comment:

  // Write a Python script to use Tesseract OCR on a batch of Fraktur images and then send the recognized text to an AI translation API

- Copilot may suggest code that imports pytesseract, iterates over a folder of images, applies OCR with a Fraktur model, and then calls an API endpoint for translation. While this is more technical, it streamlines the process so that genealogical researchers can scale up their transcription and translation efforts.

Using Gemini (Google's Next-Gen Model) for Integrated Image-to-Text-to-Translation

Functionality (Anticipated): Google's Gemini, once available, is expected to handle multimodal inputs natively, meaning it can take an image of a Fraktur record and directly provide transcription and translation. Although still forthcoming at this writing, the workflow would be simpler: upload the image, let Gemini detect the script, convert it, and produce a translated result with context.

Practical Example (Projected):

- **User Input to Gemini:**

  "Please transcribe and translate this attached image of a 19th-century Fraktur birth record into English and explain any unusual terms."

- **Expected Gemini Response: (Hypothetical)**

  Gemini provides the transcription of the name, date, place, and occupations, then translates them into English, noting that certain terms reflect historical social classes, local titles, or professions no longer in common use.

Using Perplexity AI for Cross-Referencing and Research Context

Functionality: Perplexity AI is skilled at answering queries and providing sources. Once you have a transcription and rough translation, you can query Perplexity for clarifications of historical terms and genealogical contexts. It excels as a research assistant, offering references to authoritative sources where you can verify certain interpretations of archaic language or confirm genealogical norms for the region and period in question.

Practical Example:

- **User Input to Perplexity:**

  "What does the term 'Hofbesitzer' mean in late 19th-century Bavaria, and what responsibilities did this role entail?"

- **Expected Perplexity Response:**

  A concise explanation, potentially citing historical dictionaries or genealogical research references, indicating that a "Hofbesitzer" was a farmstead owner who managed agricultural production, hired laborers, and had certain social standing within the village community.

Using Transkribus for Specialized Handwriting Recognition in Fraktur

Functionality: Transkribus is a leading platform for historical handwriting recognition. Its HTR (Handwritten Text Recognition) models are specifically trained on various historical scripts, including handwritten Fraktur, Kurrent, and Sütterlin. You can upload document scans, run the HTR engine to generate a transcription, then export that text and feed it into a general-purpose LLM like ChatGPT or Claude for translation and interpretation.

Practical Example:

- In Transkribus, load a scanned birth register page written in Fraktur by hand.

- Use the Transkribus HTR engine trained on German Fraktur handwriting to produce a line-by-line transcription.

- Export the resulting text. For instance, you get:

  "Geburt am 21ten Juni 1820, Anna Maria, Tochter des Müllermeisters Franz Meier…"

- Copy this text and paste it into ChatGPT with a prompt:

  "Please translate the following transcription from Transkribus into English and explain the occupation 'Müllermeister':

  'Geburt am 21ten Juni 1820, Anna Maria, Tochter des Müllermeisters Franz Meier…'"

- ChatGPT would respond with a translation and note that a "Müllermeister" is an expert miller, someone who owned and operated a mill, typically grinding grain into flour for the community.

Combining Multiple Tools for Best Results

A realistic genealogy workflow might look like this:

- **Transkribus:** Obtain the best possible transcription from a challenging handwritten Fraktur record.

- **LLM (ChatGPT or Claude):** Translate the raw transcription into modern German or English, clarify archaic terms, and standardize spelling.

- **Perplexity AI or Claude:** Investigate historical context, verify unusual terms, and find references to confirm interpretations of genealogical roles or addresses.

- **Copilot (Microsoft) & Scripts:** Automate the entire pipeline for larger document sets, using code suggestions to integrate OCR, HTR, and translation APIs.

- **Gemini (Future Integration):** Once released, simplify the entire workflow by processing images directly with a single multimodal AI.

* * *

By intelligently combining these major AI platforms—ChatGPT, Claude, Copilot Microsoft web-version, Gemini, Perplexity, and Transkribus—researchers can effectively tackle the challenge of reading and translating German genealogical records in Fraktur script. The right approach involves leveraging specialized OCR/HTR technology for transcription, large language models for translation and contextual understanding, and research assistants for background context. This integrated methodology streamlines the deciphering of historical documents, making the rich genealogical and cultural knowledge they contain more accessible than ever before.

Appendix 3 – Summarizing Practical Example 1 – *The Genealogy of David Putman and His Descendants*

Note: The 57-page book *The Genealogy of David Putman and His Descendants* was privately published in 1916 by G.W. Putman. Per **Practical Example 1** on page 24, the following actions were taken:

- The PDF document was split into three sections of somewhat equal length and labeled "Part 1," "Part 2," and "Part 3."

- ChatGPT versions used included 4 (free) and 4o (paid).

- Prompt **Create a detailed summary focusing on names, notable events, and locations mentioned** was used for each section.

- All three resulting summaries were combined into one "complete" summary.

- Prompt **Create a top-level summary highlighting migration trends for each family** was used uploading the complete summary.

The results for each version of ChatGPT can be found on the following pages. You can see that the paid versions of ChatGPT (4o) offer more detailed and different structures for the generative text than the free version (4).

Part 1 ChatGPT 4 prompt: *summarize this document focusing on names, notable events, and locations mentioned*

The document titled "Genealogy of David Putman and his Descendants" is a detailed family history of David Putman and various branches of his family, including numerous names, notable events, and locations:

Names Mentioned:

- David Putman: The main figure around whom the genealogy centers.

- Johannes Footman: An early ancestor with detailed records dating back to his birth in 1645.

- George W. Putman: A descendant who appears to have been involved in documenting the family history.

Notable Events:

- Several military involvements are noted, including those related to the American Revolution.

- References to various familial movements and settlements in different parts of New York such as Millville, Jordan, and Ogdensburg.

Locations:

- New York features prominently, with specific mentions of places like Schenectady, Albany, Jefferson County, and New York City.

- Other states such as Michigan and Minnesota are mentioned in the context of later family migrations.

The document provides a comprehensive look at the Putman family, tracking multiple generations and their spread across the United States, indicating significant family movements and important life events such as marriages, military service, and deaths.

Part 2 ChatGPT 4 prompt: *summarize this document focusing on names, notable events, and locations mentioned*

The document "Genealogy of David Putman and his Descendants" provides extensive information about the Putman family tree. Here's a summary of the key names, notable events, and locations mentioned:

Names:

- David Putman: Main subject of the genealogy.

- Johannes Footman: First ancestor recorded, various descendants including Victor, Aaron, Stephen, and Cornelius are mentioned.

- George W. Putman: Wrote the prefatory letter and is likely a key descendant focused on collecting the family's genealogy.

Notable Events

- Various migrations and settlements of the Putman family members in different parts of New York such as Millville, Bonfire, Jordan, Ogdensburg, and Jefferson County.

- Detailed tracking of descendants and their migrations, including their contributions to local communities, military service, and other personal achievements.

- Specific anecdotes like members being involved in military service during significant American wars.

Locations

- New York: Repeatedly mentioned as the state where many descendants lived, specifically towns like Schenectady, Albany, Millville, and Jefferson County.

- Other states such as Michigan and Pennsylvania are noted for the residences of later generations.

The document is very detailed with a lot of personal histories and connections which could be crucial for genealogical research or constructing a detailed family tree.

Part 3 ChatGPT 4 prompt: *summarize this document focusing on names, notable events, and locations mentioned*

The document "Genealogy of David Putman and his Descendants" contains a detailed account of the family history and lineage of David Putman, tracing back to an early ancestor, Johannes Footman, born in 1645. The text details various branches of the Putman family, highlighting key individuals, events, and locations significant to the family's history.

Notable Names and Events:

- David Putman: Central figure of the genealogy, with extensive details on his descendants.

- Johannes Footman: Identified as the earliest known ancestor, linked to a massacre in Schenectady where he and his wife were killed.

- George W. Putman: One section is dedicated to George and his descendants, though details are scant in the provided text.

- Various Branches: Multiple branches of the family are mentioned, such as the John branch, George Woodrow branch, and Margaret Putman Van Allen branch, each indexed with specific page references.

Locations:

- Millville, Bonfire, Cito, Jordan, Ogdensburg, and Jefferson County, NY: Places where David Putman's descendants were known to have lived or moved to.

- Schenectady, NY: Mentioned frequently as a key location in the family's history.

- New York City: Noted as a place connected to some of David Putman's military activities during the American Revolution.

The document serves as a foundational record for further detailed study into each branch and individual mentioned within the Putman family.

Compiled Section Summary Parts 1-3 ChatGPT 4 prompt: *Compile all section summaries*

The document titled "Genealogy of David Putman and his Descendants" explores the extensive family tree of David Putman, detailing the lineage from the early ancestor Johannes Footman, born in 1645, to various descendants across multiple generations. Key figures such as George W. Putman, who possibly played a significant role in compiling the family history, are highlighted alongside other descendants like Victor, Aaron, Stephen, and Cornelius. Notable events include their military involvements during the American Revolution and various familial movements and settlements across New York in places like Millville, Jordan, Ogdensburg, and more extensively in Schenectady, Albany, and Jefferson County. The family's expansion into other states like Michigan, Minnesota, and Pennsylvania is also documented. The document provides a detailed and structured account of the Putman family's history, showcasing their significant contributions to local communities, military services, and other personal achievements. This comprehensive genealogy serves as a crucial resource for understanding the family's extensive connections and historical significance.

**Compiled Section Summary Parts 1-3 ChatGPT 4
prompt: *Create a top-level summary highlighting
migration trends for each family***

The document "Genealogy of David Putman and his
Descendants" reveals distinct migration patterns within the
Putman family across several generations, highlighting a
continuous movement primarily centered in New York but
extending into other regions of the United States:

- **Initial Settlements:** The earliest known ancestor,
  Johannes Footman, and subsequent generations
  initially settled in New York, particularly in
  Schenectady and Albany, areas that remained
  central to the family for many generations.

- **Expansion within New York:** Over the years,
  descendants of David Putman spread throughout
  various parts of New York State, including Millville,
  Jordan, Ogdensburg, and Jefferson County. This
  migration trend indicates a gradual westward and
  northward expansion from their initial settlements in
  the eastern part of the state.

- **Beyond New York:** As the family grew, several
  branches began moving beyond New York to other
  states such as Michigan and Minnesota, marking a
  significant expansion into the Midwest. Pennsylvania
  was also mentioned as a new home for later
  generations, suggesting a broadening of the family's
  geographic presence in the United States.

These migration trends reflect the Putman family's
adaptation and integration into various communities, their
involvement in local industries, and military engagements
which might have influenced their movements. The
document provides a robust framework for understanding
how economic opportunities, wars, and other historical
events shaped the family's migration and settlement
patterns over the centuries.

AI and Genealogy A Practical Guide to Summarizing,
Transcribing, and Translating Historical Records

Part 1 ChatGPT 4o prompt: *create a detailed summary of this document focusing on names, notable events, and locations mentioned*

Here's a **detailed summary** focusing on **names**, **notable events**, and **locations** extracted from the genealogical document about David Putman and his descendants:

1. Key Names Mentioned

Earliest Ancestors

- **Johannes Putman/Footman (b. 1645)** - Earliest recorded ancestor, believed to be of Dutch descent. He and his wife were killed during the **Schenectady Massacre**.

Second Generation

- **Victor Putman (b. ~1680)** - Son of Johannes, married Mary Mabee, one of the oldest families in New York's Mohawk Valley.

Third Generation

- **David Putman (b. 1717 - d. March 10, 1806)** - Son of Victor, married Mary Van Antwerp. He served in the **American Revolutionary War** under Colonel Frederick Fisher in the Tryon County Militia.

- **Cornelius, Peter, Jacob, Margaret, Ahda, and Alida Putman** - His children, several of whom moved westward or played significant roles in early New York communities.

Notable Descendants in Later Generations

- **John Putman** - A farmer who lived near Tribes Hill, NY.

- **Abraham Putman** - Lived near Tribes Hill, moved to New York's frontier areas.

- **George W. Putman** - A key genealogist in the family who compiled much of the family history.

- **Alexander Utter** - Married into the family through Alida Putman, contributing to family records in Minnesota and beyond.

- **Margaret and Jacob Putman** - Played important roles in extending the family branches in various New York counties.

2. Notable Events

Historical Events

- **Schenectady Massacre (1690)** - Johannes Putman and his wife were killed, leaving their children orphaned. This event was significant in early New York history.

- **Revolutionary War Service** - Several Putman family members served in the American Revolution, especially in Tryon County, NY. David Putman's service is specifically noted in historical records.

Genealogical Research Efforts

- **Correspondence with Postmasters:** George W. Putman reached out to postmasters and local historians across New York, requesting information on family members.

- **Migration and Settlement:** Many Putman descendants moved westward into Michigan, Minnesota, and other Midwestern states during the 19th century.

3. Locations Referenced

New York State

- **Schenectady** - Where Johannes Putman first settled and died.

- **Albany County** - Early area of settlement for Putman descendants.

- **Tribes Hill, NY** - Home of David Putman and key family farms.

- **Jefferson County, NY** - Another key location for descendants.

- **Cherry Valley, NY** - Important family settlement area post-Revolutionary War.

- **Millville and Bonfire, NY** - Mentioned as early homes of descendants.

Other U.S. Locations

- **Minnesota (Swift County, St. Peter, and Benson)** - Where many descendants settled during the westward expansion.

- **Michigan (Detroit, Spirit Lake)** - Important migration stops for later family members.

- **Washington County, NY & St. Lawrence County, NY** - Additional significant settlement areas.

Part 2 ChatGPT 4o prompt: *create a detailed summary of this document focusing on names, notable events, and locations mentioned*

Based on the provided excerpts from *PART 2 Genealogy of David Putman and his Descendants*, here is a detailed summary focusing on key names, notable events, and locations:

Key Names:

- **David Putman/Pitman:** Central ancestor in the genealogy.

- **Johannes Putman/Pitman:** Earliest recorded ancestor born in 1645.

- **Victor Putman:** Second generation, born around 1680 in Schenectady, NY.

- **David Putman (son of Victor):** Born in 1717, married Sil-via Van Antwerp.

- **Abraham Putman:** Another descendant, linked to locations such as Tribes Hill, NY.

Notable Events:

- **Schenectady Massacre:** Mentioned as a critical historical event, with Johannes Putman's family affected.

- **Revolutionary War Service:** Several descendants, including David Putman, are noted for their military service during the American Revolutionary War.

- **Migration and Settlement:** The document traces the family's migration through various counties in New York and neighboring states.

Key Locations:

- **Schenectady, NY:** Central hub where early generations lived and experienced historical events.

- **Tribes Hill, NY:** A notable family settlement location.

- **Millville, NY:** Repeatedly referenced as a residence for different family members.

- **Jefferson County, NY:** Another important location tied to family history.

- **Albany, NY:** Mentioned as a place connected to Johannes Putman's descendants.

This genealogy outlines the family's expansion through New York and beyond, highlighting their personal milestones, migrations, and contributions to historical events.

Part 3 ChatGPT 4o prompt: *create a detailed summary of this document focusing on names, notable events, and locations mentioned*

Based on the content reviewed from "PART 3 Genealogy of David Putman and his Descendants," here is a detailed summary focusing on names, notable events, and locations mentioned:

AI and Genealogy A Practical Guide to Summarizing, Transcribing, and Translating Historical Records

Key Names and Family Members

- **David Putman (Pitman)**: Central figure in the genealogy, born in 1717 in Schenectady, NY. Married Silvina Van Antwerp. Noted for service during the American Revolution. His children included:
  - John Putman
  - Abraham Putman
  - Isaac Putman
  - Peter Putman
  - Jacob Putman
  - Angelica, Hannah, Margaret, and Ahda (daughters).

- **Johannes Putman (Footman)**: Earliest recorded ancestor, born in 1645. He was killed in the Schenectady Massacre of 1690.

- **Victor Putman**: Son of Johannes, born around 1680 in Schenectady, NY. Married Gunter Mabee.

- **Abraham Putman (Branch)**: Lived near Tribes Hill, NY, noted for several descendants in Montgomery and Schenectady Counties.

- **Margaret Putman Van Allen**: Another descendant line mentioned.

Notable Events

- **Schenectady Massacre (1690)**: Johannes Putman and his wife were killed during this historic event.

- **American Revolution**: David Putman served in Tryon County Militia under Colonel Frederick Fisher.

Locations Mentioned

- **Schenectady, NY**: Home of early Putman ancestors and site of the massacre.

- **Tribes Hill, NY**: Area of residence for David Putman and family.

- **Millville, Bonfire, Jordan, Ogdensburg, and Jefferson County, NY**: Locations where descendants lived and were traced.

- **Plainview, MN**: Home of some descendants later in the family history.

The genealogy includes numerous family members across generations, highlighting marriages, children, migrations, and historical contributions.

Compiled Section Summary Parts 1-3 ChatGPT 4o prompt: *Compile all section summaries*

Here is a compiled summary based on the genealogical document about David Putman and his descendants, organized by key names, notable events, and locations:

1. Key Names Mentioned

Earliest Ancestors

- **Johannes Putman/Footman (b. 1645)**: Earliest recorded ancestor, believed to be of Dutch descent. Killed with his wife during the Schenectady Massacre of 1690.

Second Generation

- **Victor Putman (b. ~1680)**: Son of Johannes, married Mary Mabee, one of the oldest families in New York's Mohawk Valley.

Third Generation

- **David Putman (b. 1717 - d. 1806)**: Son of Victor, married Mary Van Antwerp. Served in the American Revolutionary War under Colonel Frederick Fisher in the Tryon County Militia.

Children of David Putman:

- Cornelius Putman
- Peter Putman
- Jacob Putman
- Margaret Putman
- Ahda Putman
- Alida Putman

Notable Descendants in Later Generations

- **John Putman:** Farmer near Tribes Hill, NY.
- **Abraham Putman:** Migrated from Tribes Hill to New York's frontier areas.
- **George W. Putman:** Family genealogist who compiled extensive records.
- **Alexander Utter:** Married Alida Putman and contributed to family history records.
- **Margaret and Jacob Putman:** Key figures in expanding the family branches across New York counties.

2. Notable Events

Historical Events

- **Schenectady Massacre (1690):** Johannes Putman and his wife were killed, leaving their children orphaned.
- **American Revolutionary War:** Several family members, especially David Putman, served in Tryon County Militia, defending New York's frontier.

Genealogical Research Efforts

- **Family History Compilation:** George W. Putman's correspondence with postmasters and local historians helped trace family members across New York and beyond.

- **Migration and Settlement:** Family descendants migrated westward into Michigan, Minnesota, and other Midwestern states in the 19th century.

3. Locations Referenced

New York State

- **Schenectady:** Initial settlement of the Putman family and site of the Schenectady Massacre.
- **Albany County:** Early settlement region.
- **Tribes Hill, NY:** Home of David Putman and key family farms.
- **Jefferson County, Cherry Valley, Millville, and Bonfire, NY:** Important settlements for various descendants.
- **St. Lawrence and Washington Counties:** Additional locations where family members settled.

Other U.S. Locations

- **Minnesota:** Descendants settled in Swift County, St. Peter, and Benson.
- **Michigan:** Important stops for descendants, including Detroit and Spirit Lake.
- **Plainview, MN:** Mentioned in later generations' settlement history.

This compiled genealogy highlights the Putman family's roots, historical contributions, military service, migration patterns, and lasting legacy across the northeastern and midwestern United States.

Compiled Section Summary Parts 1-3 ChatGPT 4o
prompt: *Create a top-level summary highlighting*
migration trends for each family
Migration Trends of the Putman Family by Generation

1. Early Settlement (1600s-1700s)

- **Johannes Putman/Footman (b. 1645):**
  - Origin: Dutch heritage, likely immigrated from the Netherlands.
    - Settlement: Schenectady, New York (Mohawk Valley).
    - Event: Killed in the Schenectady Massacre of 1690, leaving children orphaned.

2. Second Generation (Late 1600s - Early 1700s)

- **Victor Putman (b. ~1680):**
  - Migration: Settled near Schenectady, NY, continuing the family's foothold in the Mohawk Valley.
  - Family expanded into nearby Albany County through marriage into the Mabee family.

3. Third Generation (1700s - Early 1800s)

- **David Putman (b. 1717 - d. 1806):**
  - Migration: Established farms near Tribes Hill, NY, after military service in the Revolutionary War.
  - Children spread into central New York counties, including Montgomery, Jefferson, and Schenectady.

4. Expansion into New York Frontier (Late 1700s - Early 1800s)

- **David Putman's Children:**
  - **Cornelius, Peter, Jacob, Margaret, Ahda, and Alida Putman:**

- Moved westward toward newly developing frontier towns in New York such as Cherry Valley, Millville, and Bonfire, NY.

5. Westward Migration (1800s-1900s)

- **Next Generations:**
  - **Abraham Putman:** Migrated toward New York's expanding frontier near Tribes Hill and beyond.
  - **George W. Putman:** As the family historian, he documented family branches moving into Michigan, Minnesota, and other parts of the Midwest.

6. Midwest Settlements (Mid-1800s - Early 1900s)

- **Minnesota Settlements:**
  - Descendants settled in Swift County, St. Peter, and Benson, MN.
  - **Alexander Utter and Alida Putman's descendants:** Contributed to family records from Minnesota.
- **Michigan Stops:**
  - Notable settlements included Detroit and Spirit Lake, MI, marking key westward destinations.

Summary of Migration Patterns

- **Origin:** Dutch immigration to New York (Mohawk Valley).
- **Core Settlements:** Schenectady, Tribes Hill, and surrounding NY counties.
- **Expansion:** Westward movement into Michigan, Minnesota, and the broader Midwest due to land opportunities and frontier expansion.
- **Notable Stops:** Schenectady, Albany, Tribes Hill, Cherry Valley, Jefferson County (NY); Detroit (MI); St. Peter, Swift County, and Benson (MN).

The Putman family's migration reflects a classic pattern of early Dutch settlement in New York, expansion along the Mohawk Valley, and later frontier migration driven by land availability and family growth.

Appendix 4 – Transcribing Practical Example 1 – *Drowned at Long Beach*

Note: The death notice **Drowned at Long Beach** about the death of Robert Austin was published in The Lowville Journal Republican on 24 September 1924.

DROWNED AT LONG BEACH .

Robert Austin, Formerly of Lowville,
Loses Life on Labor Day
While Bathing.

Robert Austin, 30, son of Mr. and Mrs. William D. Austin, formerly of Lowville, was drowned at Long Beach, L. I., Monday, but no particulars of the accident are at hand. The Austin family removed from this village to New York several years ago. Robert Austin was born here October 13, 1894. At the time of his death he held the responsible position of office manager for the D. W. Griffith Motion Picture Corporation, being in charge of the New York office. He was married about two years ago. Besides his wife and parents he leaves four brothers, Maurice, Harry, Ralph and Lawton, all of New York city.

Per **Practical Example 1** on page 31, the following actions were taken:

- The newspaper clipping was scanned and saved as JPG image.

- The JPG was uploaded to ChatGPT.

- ChatGPT versions used included 4 (free) and 4o (paid).

- Prompt: *transcribe exactly including line breaks as shown in image*.

The results for each version of ChatGPT can be found on the following pages. You can see that the paid version of ChatGPT (4o) offered more detailed and different structures for the generative text than the free version (4).

Transcription ChatGPT 4 (free) prompt:
Transcribe exactly including line breaks as shown in image

DROWNED AT LONG BEACH
Robert Austin, Formerly of Lowville,
Loses Life on Labor Day
While Bathing.

Robert Austin, 30, son of Mr. and
Mrs. William D. Austin, formerly of
Lowville, was drowned at Long Beach,
L. I., Monday, but no particulars of
the accident are at hand. The Austin
family removed from this village to
New York several years ago. Robert
Austin was born here October 13,
1894. At the time of his death he had
the responsible position of office
manager in the D.W. Griffith Motion
Picture Corporation. Being in charge
of the New York office, he was married about ten years ago. Besides his
wife and parents he leaves four brothers, Maurice, Harry, Ralph and Walton, all of New York city.

Note: the name "Lawton" at the end of the article was transcribed as "Walton."

AI and Genealogy A Practical Guide to Summarizing, Transcribing, and Translating Historical Records

Transcription ChatGPT 4o (paid) prompt:
Transcribe exactly including line breaks as shown in image

DROWNED AT LONG BEACH
Robert Austin, Formerly of Lowville,
Loses Life on Labor Day
While Bathing.

Robert Austin, 30, son of Mr. and
Mrs. William D. Austin, formerly of
Lowville, was drowned at Long Beach,
L. I., Monday, but no particulars of
the accident are at hand. The Austin
family removed from this village to
New York several years ago. Robert
Austin was born here October 13,
1894. At the time of his death he held
the responsible position of office
manager for the D. W. Griffith Motion
Picture Corporation, being in charge
of the New York office. He was married about two years ago. Besides a
wife and parents he leaves four brothers, Maurice, Harry, Ralph and Lawton, all of New York city.

AI and Genealogy A Practical Guide to Summarizing, Transcribing, and Translating Historical Records

Appendix 5 – Transcribing Practical Example 2 – *Certificate of Baptism of Barbara Jacqueline Austin*

Note: The certificate of baptism form for Barbara Jacqueline Austin was completed with handwriting and dated 27 August 1958.

Per **Practical Example 2** on page 31, the following actions were taken:

- The certificate was scanned and saved as JPG image.

- The JPG was uploaded to ChatGPT.

- ChatGPT versions used included 4 (free) and 4o (paid).

- Prompt: *transcribe exactly*.

The results for each version of ChatGPT can be found on the following pages. You can see that the paid version of ChatGPT (4o) offered more detailed and different structures for the generative text than the free version (4).

Transcription ChatGPT 4 (free) prompt: *Transcribe exactly*

Certificate of Baptism

Church of **The Blessed Sacrament** 152 W 71 St. N.Y.C.

This is to Certify

That **Barbara Jacqueline Austin**,
Child of **Clifford Austin**
and **Eula Wenberg**
born in N.Y.C.
on the **12th** day of **July 1941** was Baptized
on the **21st** day of **September 1941**
According to the Rite of the Roman Catholic Church
by the Rev. **B. T. Carrigy**
the Sponsors being **Anthony Marconi**
and **Ethel Marconi** as appears from
the Baptismal Register of this Church.

AI and Genealogy A Practical Guide to Summarizing, Transcribing, and Translating Historical Records

Dated August 27, 1945

[signature]
Rev. W. A. Cullen, Pastor.

NO. 214N © D. P. MURPHY CO., NEW YORK

Notes:

- The father's name – Alfred Austin – was transcribed as Clifford Austin

- The mother's name – Anna Henneberg – was transcribed as Eula Wenberg

- The priest's name – B.F. Conray – was transcribed as B.T. Carrigy

- The date August 27, 1958 was transcribed as August 27, 1945

Transcription ChatGPT 4o (paid) prompt: *Transcribe exactly*

Certificate of Baptism

Church of
The Blessed Sacrament
152 W 71 St NYC

This is to Certify

That **Barbara Jacqueline Austin**
Child of **Alfred Austin**
and **Anna Henneberg**

born in **NYC**
on the **12th day of July 1941** was Baptized
on the **21st day of September 1941**

According to the Rite of the Roman Catholic Church
by the **Rev. B.J. Conraiz**
the Sponsors being **Anthony Marconi**
and **Ethel Marconi** as appears from
the Baptismal Register of this Church.

Dated **August 27, 1952**

Pastor: *(Signature appears here)*

Notes:

- The priest's name – B.F. Conray – was transcribed as B.T. Conraiz

- The date August 27, 1958 was transcribed as August 27, 1952

Appendix 6 – Transcribing Practical Example 3 – *Handwritten Affidavit of Ebenezer Horsam dated 1819*

Note: The handwritten affidavit of Ebenezer Horsam dated 17 July 1819 in support of application for a Revolutionary War Pension downloaded from the National Archives and Records Administration.

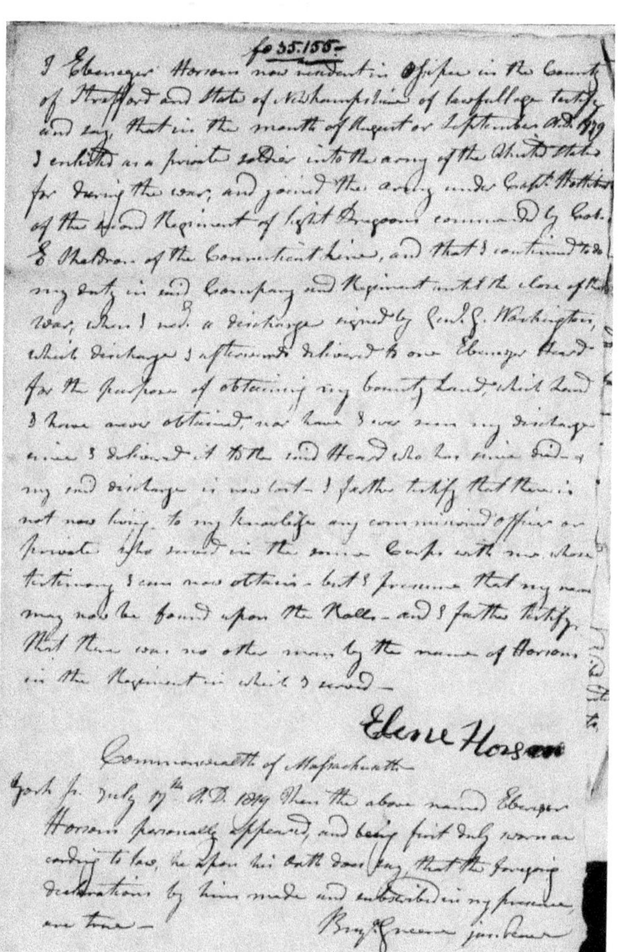

Per **Practical Example 3** on page 31, the following actions were taken:

- The letter was downloaded from the National Archives and Records Administration and saved as JPG image.

- The JPG was uploaded to ChatGPT.

- ChatGPT versions used included 4 (free) and 4o (paid).

- Prompt: ***transcribe exactly this handwritten affidavit of Ebenezer Horsam dated 17 July 1819 as part of a US Revolutionary War Pension file***.

The results for each version of ChatGPT can be found on the following pages. You can see that the paid version of ChatGPT (4o) offered more detailed and different structures for the generative text than the free version (4).

Transcription ChatGPT 4 (free) prompt: *Transcribe exactly this handwritten affidavit of Ebenezer Horsam dated 17 July 1819 as part of a US Revolutionary War Pension file*

No. 55.135

I Ebenezer Horsam now resident in Goffstown in the County of Strafford State of New Hampshire of lawful age testify and say that in the month of August or there abouts in the year 1779 I enlisted as a private Soldier into the service of the United States for during the war, and joined the army under Capt. Hattin of the 2d Regiment of light Dragoons commanded by Col. Elisha Sheldon of the Connecticut line, and that I continued in my duty in said company as a private in the care of the said Capt. when I had a discharge regularly (said discharge which discharge is afforesaid delivered to our Colonel that day for the purpose of obtaining my bounty land, which land I have never obtained, nor have I ever seen my discharge since 3 January 1780. I heard it was in said Col. my said discharge it was lost - by the faithless Postmaster in not delivering to my knowledge my commissioned officer an honest justifiable service. The said Capt. with whom I have had that business I can now obtain but its presumed that my discharge may still be found upon the Rolls, as I have the Discharge that was was to other men by the names of Horton etc in the Revolution that is now in—

Elias Horsam

Commonwealth of Massachusetts Goffstown. July 17, 1819. Then the above named Ebenezer Horsam personally appeared and made oath that the foregoing declaration by him made and subscribed is just and true. Before me, Bayliese, Jus. Peace

Notes: see highlighted errors below

No. 55.135

I Ebenezer Horsam now resident in ~~Goffstown~~ in the County of Strafford State of New Hampshire of lawful age testify and say that in the month of August ~~or there abouts~~ **September** in the year 1779 I enlisted as a private Soldier into the ~~service~~ **army** of the United States for during the war, and joined the army under Capt. ~~Hattin~~ **?** of the ~~2d~~ **Second** Regiment of light Dragoons commanded by Col. ~~Elisha~~ **E.** Sheldon of the Connecticut line, and that I continued **to do** ~~in~~ my duty in said company ~~as a private in the care of the said Capt.~~ **and Regiment until the close of that war** when I had a discharge ~~regularly (said discharge~~ signed by General G. Washington which discharge is aforesaid delivered to ~~our~~ **one** E. Heard ~~that day~~ for the purpose of obtaining my bounty land, which land I have never obtained, nor have I ever seen my discharge since **I delivered it to the to the said Heard** ~~3 January 1780~~ ~~I heard it was in said Col.~~ who has since died **my said** discharge it was lost. **I further testify that there is no not now living to my knowledge any commissioned officer or private who served in the same Corps as me whose testimony** ~~by the faithless Postmaster in not delivering to my knowledge my~~ ~~an honest justifiable service. The said Capt. with whom I have had that business~~ I can now obtain but ~~its~~ I presume that my ~~discharge~~ name may ~~still~~ now be found upon the Rolls – and I further testifythat there was no other man ~~, as I have the Discharge that was was to other men~~ by the names of Horsam ~~etc in the Revolution~~ ~~that is now in~~ **in the Regiment in which I served.**

~~Elias~~ Ebenezer Horsam

Commonwealth of Massachusetts ~~Goffstown~~ **?** July 17**th**, 1819 **A.D.** Then the above named Ebenezer Horsam personally appeared and **being first duly sworn as coming according to law**, ~~made~~ **he upon this** oath **does say** that the foregoing declaration**s** by him made and subscribed **in my presence** ~~is just and~~ are true. ~~Before me, Bayliese, ?~~ Jus. Peace

AI and Genealogy A Practical Guide to Summarizing, Transcribing, and Translating Historical Records

Transcription ChatGPT 4o (paid) prompt: *Transcribe exactly this handwritten affidavit of Ebenezer Horsam dated 17 July 1819 as part of a US Revolutionary War Pension file*

No. 25.155.
I Ebenezer Horsam now resident in Oxford in the
County of Worcester and State of Massachusetts of
lawful age testify and say that in the month of August
or September A.D. 1779 I enlisted as a private
soldier into the army of the United States for during
the war, and joined the army under Capt. Matthias of
the Second Regiment of Light Dragoons commanded
by Col. Sheldons of the Connecticut line, and that I
continued to do my duty in said Company and
Regiment until the close of the war, when I rec'd a
discharge signed (Indt.) Washington, which
discharge I afterward delivered to one Ebenezer
Read for the purpose of obtaining my bounty land,
which land I have never obtained nor have I ever
seen my discharge since I delivered it to the said
Read who has since died. & my said discharge is
now lost. I further testify that there is not now living to
my knowledge any commissioned officer or private
who served in the same Corps with me whose
testimony I can now obtain but I presume that my
name may now be found upon the Rolls and I further
testify that there was no other man by the name of
Horsam in the Regiment in which I served.

Ebenezer Horsam

Commonwealth of Massachusetts
Oxford ss. July 17th A.D. 1819 Then the above
named Ebenezer Horsam personally appeared and
being first duly sworn according to law, he upon his
oath doth say that the foregoing declaration by him

made and subscribed is in his presence and time.
Benjn Green Justice of Peace

Notes: see highlighted errors below

No. 25.155.
I Ebenezer Horsam now resident in ~~Oxford~~ **Ossipee**
in the County of ~~Worcester~~ **Stafford** and State of
~~Massachusetts~~ **New Hampshire** of lawful age testify
and say that in the month of August or September
A.D. 1779 I enlisted as a private soldier into the army
of the United States for during the war, and joined
the army under Capt. Matthias of the Second
Regiment of Light Dragoons commanded by Col. **E**
Sheldons of the Connecticut line, and that I
continued to do my duty in said Company and
Regiment until the close of the war, when I rec'd a
discharge signed ~~(Indt.)~~ by **General George**
Washington, which discharge I afterward delivered to
one Ebenezer ~~Read~~ **Heard** for the purpose of
obtaining my bounty land, which land I have never
obtained nor have I ever seen my discharge since I
delivered it to the said ~~Read~~ **Heard** who has since
died. & my said discharge is now lost. I further testify
that there is not now living to my knowledge any
commissioned officer or private who served in the
same Corps with me whose testimony I can now
obtain but I presume that my name may now be
found upon the Rolls and I further testify that there
was no other man by the name of Horsam in the
Regiment in which I served.

Ebenezer Horsam

Commonwealth of Massachusetts
Oxford ss. July 17th A.D. 1819 Then the above
named Ebenezer Horsam personally appeared and
being first duly sworn according to law, he upon his

Al and Genealogy A Practical Guide to Summarizing,
Transcribing, and Translating Historical Records

oath doth say that the foregoing declaration**s** by him
made and subscribed ~~is~~ in ~~his~~ **my** presence ~~and time~~
are true.
Benjn Green Justice of Peace

Note: *Thanks to Barbara J. Beake of the Essex Society of
Genealogists (https://www.esog.org/) in Lynnfield,
Massachusetts for her knowledge of Ossipee, New
Hampshire and assisting with the errors found in the
transcription generated in ChatGPT Version 4o.*

AI and Genealogy A Practical Guide to Summarizing, Transcribing, and Translating Historical Records

Appendix 7 – Translating Practical Example 1 – *Le troisième centenaire de l'Édit de Nantes en Amérique et en France*

Note: The book *Le troisième centenaire de l'Édit de Nantes en Amérique et en France* was published in 1898 and a JPG image was created from a PDF downloaded from the Internet Archive website.

2   LE TROISIÈME CENTENAIRE DE L'ÉDIT DE NANTES.

résolut, dans l'article V de ses statuts, de tenir chaque année son assemblée générale, le 13 avril, « jour anniversaire de la promulga- « tion de l'édit de Nantes qui accorda la liberté de culte aux hugue- « nots de France ». Lors de son dernier voyage en Europe, en octobre 1894, Mrs. Lawton se mit en rapport avec les Sociétés hugue- notes de Paris et de Londres, et c'est dès le mois de février 1897 qu'elle leur fit parvenir l'invitation officielle que ce *Bulletin* a repro- duite dans son numéro du 15 octobre de la même année. Des deux délégués désignés par notre Société d'Histoire pour répondre à cette invitation, un seul, le soussigné, a pu se rendre à New-York — et, par conséquent, c'est lui seul qui est chargé de résumer ici ses impressions.

New-York et la Huguenot Society.

Un mot d'abord sur la ville, le pays et la Société huguenote. J'avais visité les États-Unis, une première fois, il y a tantôt vingt- cinq ans, en automne 1873[1], et j'en étais revenu très frappé par les ressources inépuisables, le caractère éminemment entreprenant, l'activité juvénile, dédaigneuse des apparences, du nouveau conti- nent et de ses habitants. New-York était alors une grande ville très remuante, déjà riche, mais aux rues mal tenues, aux devantures peu attrayantes, faisant souvent l'effet d'un bazar ou d'un chantier et ne soutenant décidément pas la comparaison avec Paris ou Londres. Aujourd'hui, il ne faut pas se le dissimuler, la métropole des États-Unis entre en concurrence avec celles du vieux monde, non seulement pour les ressources, l'activité prodigieuse, mais encore en ce qui concerne l'aspect extérieur. Les rues et avenues de New-York sont à peu près aussi bien tenues que celles de Paris ou de Londres, les magasins luxueux aux vitrines artistiques, les maisons monumentales, les églises souvent remarquables au point de vue architectural y foisonnent, et Central Park tend à devenir une succursale transatlantique du bois de Boulogne. Il y a même des musées dont certaines toiles ou collections ne le cèdent en rien aux plus belles du continent. Et, pour être juste, il faut ajouter que, d'une manière générale, le pauvre et le riche vivent et circulent plus aisément, plus rapidement et plus confortablement à New-York

1. On trouvera mes impressions de cette époque dans *Le Naufrage de la Ville-du-Havre et du Loch-Earn, Souvenirs personnels par N. Weiss*, Paris, Société des Écoles du Dimanche, 1 vol. in-18 de 182 pages, 1874.

Per **Practical Example 2** on page 38, the following actions were taken:

- Scan the book page and save as JPG image. Or download a PDF of the book and create a JPG image of page 2.

- Upload the image to ChatGPT.

- Use prompt ***Translate this page from Le troisième centenaire de l'Édit de Nantes en Amérique et en France published 1898 from French to English***

- Proof and check generative text for errors.

Translation ChatGPT 4 (free) prompt: *Translate this page from Le troisième centenaire de l'Édit de Nantes en Amérique et en France published 1898 from French to English*

The Third Centenary of the Edict of Nantes

In Article V of its statutes, it resolved to hold its annual general meeting on April 13, the anniversary of the promulgation of the Edict of Nantes, which granted freedom of worship to the Huguenots of France. During her last trip to Europe in October 1894, Mrs. Lawton made contact with the Huguenot societies of Paris and London, and it was in February 1897 that she managed to have the official invitation, which the *Bulletin* reproduced in its October 15 issue of the same year. Of the two delegates appointed by our Historical Society to respond to this invitation, only one, the undersigned, was able to travel to New York—and therefore, it is he alone who is charged with summarizing here his impressions.

AI and Genealogy A Practical Guide to Summarizing, Transcribing, and Translating Historical Records

New York and the Huguenot Society

Firstly, a word on the city, the country, and the Huguenot Society. I had visited the United States for the first time nearly twenty-five years ago, in the autumn of 1873, and I was struck by its inexhaustible resources, its markedly entrepreneurial spirit, the youthfulness and disdain for appearances, which continue to characterize the city and its inhabitants. New York was then already a very wealthy city, but with poorly maintained streets, creating the impression of a bazaar or construction site, which decisively does not compare with Paris or London. Today, one must not shy away from acknowledging the metropolis that the United States has become, not only in terms of resources and prodigious activity, but also in terms of outward appearance. The streets and avenues of New York are almost as well-kept as those of Paris or London, the luxury shops with artistic window displays, monumental buildings, and churches often so remarkable from an architectural viewpoint flourish, and Central Park is becoming a transatlantic counterpart to the Bois de Boulogne. There is even a museum where certain paintings and collections are second to none on the continent. And to be fair, it must be added that, generally speaking, the poor and the rich live and move more easily, quickly, and comfortably in New York than elsewhere.

You can find my impressions of this period in Le Naufrage de la Ville-du-Havre et du Loch-Earn, Personal Souvenirs by N. Weiss, Paris, Société des Écoles du Dimanche, 1 vol. in-18 of 182 pages, 1874.

Notes: no obvious errors

Translation ChatGPT 4o (paid) prompt:
Translate this page from Le troisième centenaire de l'Édit de Nantes en Amérique et en France published 1898 from French to English

The Third Centenary of the Edict of Nantes

Resolved, in Article V of its statutes, to hold its general assembly each year on April 13, "the anniversary of the promulgation of the Edict of Nantes, which granted freedom of worship to the Huguenots of France." During her last trip to Europe in October 1894, Mrs. Lawton established connections with the Huguenot societies of Paris and London. In February 1897, she forwarded them the official invitation reproduced in this Bulletin in its issue of October 15 of the same year. Of the two delegates designated by our Historical Society to respond to this invitation, only one, the undersigned, was able to travel to New York and, consequently, it is solely upon me to summarize my impressions here.

New York and the Huguenot Society

A word first about the city, the country, and the Huguenot Society.
I had visited the United States for the first time nearly twenty-five years ago, in the autumn of 1873, and I had been deeply struck by its inexhaustible resources, the eminently enterprising character, the youthful dynamism, disdain for appearances, and the newness of the continent and its inhabitants. At that time, New York was already a bustling, wealthy city, but with poorly maintained streets, unattractive storefronts, often giving the impression of a bazaar or

a construction site, and definitely not comparable to Paris or London.

Today, we must acknowledge that the metropolis of the United States competes with the old world not only in resources and remarkable activity but also in terms of its external appearance. The streets and avenues of New York are almost as well-maintained as those of Paris or London; the luxurious stores with artistic window displays, monumental buildings, and architecturally rich churches abound. Central Park is tending to become a transatlantic counterpart of the Bois de Boulogne. There are even museums with paintings or collections that rival the finest on the continent.

And to be fair, it should also be noted that, generally speaking, the poor and the rich live and move more easily, more quickly, and more comfortably in New York.

Notes: There are some slight stylistic differences compared to the 4 (free) version of ChatGPT.

Appendix 8 – Translating Practical Example 2 – *German Marriage Record*

Nr. 28

Vor dem unterzeichneten Standesbeamten erschien heute zum Zweck der Eheschließung:

1. der Tagelöhner Valentin [illegible]

der Persönlichkeit nach [illegible] bekannt,

[illegible] Religion, geboren den [illegible] des Jahres tausend acht hundert [illegible] zu [illegible], wohnhaft zu Bitterfeld,

[illegible]

Sohn des Tagelöhner Johann [illegible] und seiner Ehefrau Sophie geb. [illegible], [illegible] wohnhaft zu Bitterfeld,

2. die Tagelöhnerin Antonie [illegible] geb. Weiss

der Persönlichkeit nach [illegible] bekannt,

[illegible] Religion, geboren den [illegible] des Jahres tausend acht hundert [illegible] zu [illegible], wohnhaft zu [illegible]

[illegible]

Tochter des [illegible] Anton Weiss und seiner Ehefrau Marianne geb. [illegible], [illegible] wohnhaft zu [illegible]

Per **Practical Example 2** on page 38, the following actions were taken:

- Scan the document and save it as JPG image.

- Transcribe the German text using ChatGPT with this prompt: ***transcribe exactly this German marriage record***.

- Check the transcribed text against the original.

- Copy the transcribed text and paste it into ChatGPT with this prompt: ***translate exactly this German text from a marriage record***.

- Check the translated text against the original.

Translation ChatGPT 4 (free) prompt:
Transcribe exactly this German marriage record and ***Translate exactly this German text from a marriage record***

Nr. 29 B.

Heiraths-Act am zwanzigsten Oktober tausend acht hundert achtzig und sechs

Vor dem unterzeichneten Standesbeamten erschienen heute zum Zweck der Eheschließung:

1. der Tagelöhner Valentin Antkowiak der Persönlichkeit nach bekannt, katholischer Religion, geboren den zweiundzwanzigsten April des Jahres tausend acht hundert zu Koscierzyna, wohnhaft zu Rützow,

unverehelicht, Sohn der Tagelöhner Thomas Antkowiak und dessen Ehefrau Anna geborene Sydow, wohnhaft zu Rützow,

2. die Wilhelmine Franczowiak der Persönlichkeit nach bekannt, katholischer Religion, geboren den fünfundzwanzigsten September des

AI and Genealogy A Practical Guide to Summarizing, Transcribing, and Translating Historical Records

Jahres tausend acht hundert zu Cadinen, wohnhaft zu Rützow,

unverehelicht, Tochter des Tagelöhner Ulrich Franczowiak und dessen Ehefrau Anna geborene Meyer, wohnhaft zu Cadinen.

and

No. 29 B.

Marriage Act on the twentieth October one thousand eight hundred eighty-six

Before the undersigned registrar appeared today for the purpose of marriage:

1. the day laborer Valentin Antkowiak personally known, of Catholic religion, born on the twenty-second April of the year one thousand eight hundred in Koscierzyna, residing in Rützow,

unmarried, son of the day laborer Thomas Antkowiak and his wife Anna née Sydow, residing in Rützow,

2. Wilhelmine Franczowiak personally known, of Catholic religion, born on the twenty-fifth September of the year one thousand eight hundred in Cadinen, residing in Rützow,

unmarried, daughter of the day laborer Ulrich Franczowiak and his wife Anna née Meyer, residing in Cadinen.

Translation ChatGPT 4o (paid) prompt:
Transcribe exactly this German marriage record
and *Translate exactly this German text from a
marriage record*

Nr. 28
Kirspaur am dreißigsten Oktober tausend acht
hundert acht und neunzig

Vor dem unterzeichneten Standesbeamten erschien
heute zum
Zweck der Eheschließung:

1. der Tagelöhner Valentin Antkowiak
   der Persönlichkeit nach _______________
   bekannt,
   katholischer Religion, geboren den zwei und
   dreißigsten Januar des Jahres tausend acht
   hundert ein und siebzig zu Kirsen,
   wohnhaft zu Ritterfeld,
   Sohn des Tagelöhners Johann Antkowiak und
   dessen Ehefrau Sophie, geb. Poko,
   beide zuletzt wohnhaft zu Kirsen.

2. die Tagelöhnerin Antonie Wiza, geb. Wiese,
   der Persönlichkeit nach _______________
   bekannt,
   katholischer Religion, geboren den siebenten
   September des Jahres tausend acht hundert
   sieben und siebzig zu Karmun,
   wohnhaft zu Ritterfeld,
   Tochter des Tagelöhners Anton Wiese und
   dessen Ehefrau Marianne, geb. Sikorski,
   beide verstorben zuletzt wohnhaft zu Karmun.

and

No. 28
Kirspaur, on the thirtieth of October, one thousand
eight hundred and ninety-eight

AI and Genealogy A Practical Guide to Summarizing,
Transcribing, and Translating Historical Records

Before the undersigned registrar appeared today for the purpose of marriage:

1. The day laborer Valentin Antkowiak, personally known ________________, of Catholic religion, born on the thirty-second of January of the year one thousand eight hundred and seventy-one in Kirsen, residing in Ritterfeld, son of the day laborer Johann Antkowiak and his wife Sophie, née Poko, both last residing in Kirsen.

2. The day laborer Antonie Wiza, née Wiese, personally known ________________, of Catholic religion, born on the seventh of September of the year one thousand eight hundred and seventy-seven in Karmun, residing in Ritterfeld, daughter of the day laborer Anton Wiese and his wife Marianne, née Sikorski, both deceased, last residing in Karmun.

Note: It appears that version 4 (free) of ChatGPT made several errors in transcription as well as translation when compared to the text generated by version 4o (paid). This is actually typical of using the free version and a "fill in the blank" form with handwriting.

- "October 20th" (4) instead of "October 30th" (4o)

- "Wilhelmine Franczowiak" (4) instead of "Antonie Wiza, née Wiese" (4o)

- "Ulrich Franczowiak and his wife Anna née Meyer" (4) instead of "daughter of the day laborer **Anton Wiese and his wife** Marianne, **née** Sikorski"

- Also note that 4o created an editor's note about a mistake in the original – the date 32nd of January instead of 22nd.

AI and Genealogy A Practical Guide to Summarizing, Transcribing, and Translating Historical Records

About The Author

So, what if I told you that a Baby Boomer guy with a love of punk rock music but also Renaissance Art, somehow "fell" into the technology industry almost 40 years ago, and then left a lucrative career in information technology to pursue his love of family history and genealogy?

And that his passion for tracing his roots began almost 50 years ago when he was watching the mini-series Roots on ABC Television at his great-grandparents' house in February 1977?

While some might think these two elements - technology and historical research – are opposites. The truth is, "tech people" like Thomas are needed to guide today's genealogists through the maze of options so they can deploy the best apps and devices as they break down those research brick walls.

Having taught over 1,000 in-person and virtual genealogy lectures since 2010, serving on the boards of many genealogical societies, organizing a group of over 1,000 genealogy bloggers, and helping researchers save money on genealogy products and services, Thomas is ready for the next chapter in his professional journey: changing the way genealogists acquire new research skills, motivating researchers to take a chance on new technologies, and improving how family stories and heirlooms are preserved and passed on to the next generations.